Internet Virtual Worlds Quick Tour

MUDs, MOOs & MUSHes: Interactive Games, Conferences & Forums

Internet Virtual Worlds Quick Tour

MUDs, MOOs & MUSHes: Interactive Games, Conferences & Forums

Sean Carton

Ventana Press

Internet Virtual Worlds Quick Tour: MUDs, MOOs & MUSHes: Interactive Games, Conferences & Forums

Library of Congress Cataloging-in-Publication Data

Book design: Marcia Webb
Cover design: Dawne Sherman
Cover illustration: Dawne Sherman
Vice President, Ventana Press: Walter R. Bruce III
Art Director: Marcia Webb
Design staff: Dawne Sherman, Mike Webster
Editorial Manager: Pam Richardson
Editorial staff: Angela Anderson, Tracye Giles, Nathaniel Mund
Developmental Editor: Tim C. Mattson
Project Editor: Jessica Ryan
Print Department: Wendy Bernhardt, Dan Koeller
Product Manager: Clif McCormick
Production Manager: John Cotterman
Production staff: Patrick Berry
Index service: Dianne Bertsch, Answers Plus
Proofreader: Martin V. Minner
Technical review: Matthew Saderholm

First Edition 9 8 7 6 5 4 3 2 1
Printed in the United States of America

Ventana Press, Inc.
P.O. Box 2468
Chapel Hill, NC 27515
919/942-0220
FAX 919/942-1140

TRADEMARKS

About the Author

Sean Carton is a writer, graphics specialist, Internet consultant and compulsive netsurfer. He has contributed to *bOING bOING* (the world's greatest neurozine) and *Link* magazines. His book publishing credits include coauthoring with Gareth Branwyn the *Mosaic Quick Tour* series (Ventana Press, 1995), covering MUDs and MOOs for Ventana Press's *Internet Roadside Attractions* (Ventana Press, 1995) and providing assorted Net-mischief for *bOING bOING's Happy Mutant Handbook* (Putnam Berkeley, 1995). In addition to writing and holding down a job managing a color service bureau, Sean consults on Internet marketing matters and does a bit of World Wide Web site development. He's been on the Net for about 7 years—a long time if you're a dog.

Acknowledgments

The big hero of this book is my wife, Lorna. She put up with a whole lot of short weekends, late nights and grumpy mornings so that I could bring you this book. I never could have made it without her.

I'd also like to thank my wonderful friend, Gareth Branwyn. He's totally responsible for getting me here, and his constant and unwavering support, strength and friendship kept me going. Thanks, Gar!

Thanks to my family—my parents, Bob and Christy Carton, and my sister, Tina. If my folks hadn't chipped in to help me buy that first computer 12 years ago, I'd probably be driving monster trucks at the Frederick Fairgrounds. (I'm just kidding! I'd probably opt for the tractor pull.)

A tip o' the hat to two people who helped me with some of the hairier details of the book: Charles "Nigel" Lavin, gamer extraordinaire, for his sage advice, and Jim Timmons, my generous father-in-law, for providing me with some much-needed hardware in a pinch.

I'd like to offer my heartfelt thanks to my editor, Jessica Ryan. Even through her flu and my greenhorn bungles, she still managed to drag this whole thing together. Thanks Jess!

Finally, I want to thank all the tireless people who create, maintain and keep improving all the wonderful worlds on the Net. Your worlds make this world a much more interesting place to live.

CONTENTS

INTRODUCTION

There's a whole new universe out there.

Today, thousands of people all over the globe are visiting, building, playing and getting together on virtual worlds—text-based virtual realities where anything can happen (and often does!). From online conference centers to virtual communities, from adventure games to fantastic fantasy lands, virtual worlds are some of the most exciting places on the Internet. In the past, visiting these worlds often meant learning a lot of obscure commands, deciphering cryptic Internet addresses and dealing with the greatest problem of all—fear of the unknown.

The key to this new universe is in your hands. In this book you'll learn how to find and connect to these new worlds and what to do once you've arrived. We'll look at the basics of creating an effective online persona, how to interact with other people you meet and how to thrive and survive while you're online. You'll discover the difference between MUDs and MOOs and even pick up some of the lingo you'll need to become a real virtual world veteran. We'll cover the basic commands you need to get around and some nifty tips and tricks to make your virtual life easier. For you creative types, we'll even cover some MOO programming as we build our own online house, complete with furniture! During our travels, we'll dig deep into the history of the online world to find out just where these worlds came from and who's responsible for creating them. There's even an online atlas and travel guide so you can plan your travels on the Net!

There's a lot of territory to cover, so let's get started. You may be wondering what you need to get started on your adventures. Let's find out.

Necessary Connections

One of the coolest things about visiting virtual worlds is that you don't need any fancy gear to get there. Because most of these worlds are built out of text and your imagination, you can access them with just about the simplest set up. All you need is

- A computer. Just about any kind will do as long as you've got a monitor and a keyboard attached.
- A modem. Since we aren't dealing with a bunch of fancy graphics, even a 2400 baud modem will get you there.
- A connection to the Internet. Again, you don't need anything too swanky. As long as you have access to some of the most basic Net services—telnet and FTP—you can log onto virtual worlds.

Note: Some of the big online services like to say they allow you "access to the Internet." However, most of the time this means that you can send e-mail, read USENET news, and maybe use FTP to transfer files. It usually doesn't mean you can use telnet, the one tool you need to access the various worlds online. Read the fine print—if your service doesn't offer telnet, find one that does before you go any further.

That's the basics. Of course, if you already have a SLIP or PPP connection, that'll work fine too but it's not necessary. As long as you have access to the Internet, the keys to the virtual universe are yours!

How to Use *Internet Virtual Worlds Quick Tour*

This book was written for people who've never visited a virtual world. Even though we'll cover some of the basics of using the Internet to snag some files and connect to other computers, if you're new to the Net, you'll want to grab a good beginners Internet guide to use as a reference when you need some Net help. Ventana's *Internet Tour Guide* series or the *Internet Membership Kit* (both from Ventana Press, 1995) are great places to start.

Because this is a guide for beginners, I've tried to keep it simple. Today, there are more virtual worlds on the Net than you can shake several sticks at. Trying to cover all of them in detail would have been next to impossible and would have made a book that you'd need a forklift just to get off the shelf. I've tried to limit the confusion (and the weight of this book!) by sticking to the basics—how to connect, create a character and get around. As you venture out into the virtual universe, you may find that some commands on some worlds might be a bit different than what you find in this book. Don't worry! If you follow the examples closely and learn how to use the help command, you'll be prepared for anything that comes your way.

The best way to use this book is to think of it as advice from a well-traveled friend. Even though your experiences may be different when we visit the same places, if you read carefully you'll at least know the best way to get there, what major landmarks you should visit, what clothes to pack and what hazards you might encounter on your journey.

What's Inside

Chapter 1, "Life, Death & Adventure on the Net," is a quick overview of what awaits you on a virtual world. We'll jump right in with a first-person look at what your first few minutes on a MUD might be like. Then, we'll cover a brief history of the online world and finally, we'll take a quick peek at the different types of worlds out there on the Net.

Chapter 2, "Getting Connected" is your Internet boot-camp. We'll go through all the basics—what kind of connection you need to get online, what kinds of programs you need to connect to virtual worlds and how to use what you've learned to actually get online and connect to your first MUD. Along the way, we'll delve into telnet, FTP and several MUD "clients" as we examine some of the tools of the trade.

In Chapter 3, "Getting In the Game," we'll roll up our virtual sleeves and get to work—we'll log onto a real MUD, create a character, gather some goods and maybe even get into a bit of adventure!

Chapter 4, "MUDs: Multiplayer Adventures," guides you through some of the nitty gritty of adventure on a virtual world. You'll learn just what makes one type of world different from another, how to make a name for yourself online, how to get around on an online world and what to do when you find yourself thrust into combat for the first time. Look for the list of crucial MUD strategies and tips, it's sure to make your online life just a bit easier.

Chapter 5, "Virtual Communities: MOOs, MUCKs & MUSHes," examines the other side of the virtual universe. We'll learn about online communities where you can hang out, meet people and even build your own online home. We'll log onto a MOO, create a character and even try our hands at some MOO programming!

Chapter 6, "Online Etiquette," covers a much-overlooked part of becoming a responsible member of any virtual community you visit. You'll learn how to conduct yourself as a newbie and how to make sure that little misunderstandings now don't become big problems in the future. This chapter is a must-read for anyone who spends any time online.

Chapter 7, "The Future," examines how some of the cutting-edge technologies of today are quickly becoming the standards for the future. We'll look at some really cool experiments where people are using the power of the World Wide Web to bring graphics to text-based virtual reality, as well as some nifty glimpses into how the online worlds of today might become the virtual conference centers and universities of the future.

Chapter 8, "Online Atlas & Travel Guide," helps plan your trip with a look at over 25 of the coolest virtual worlds you could ever want to visit. I've divided them into several sections, so finding a world that suits your fancy should be no problem. It's a big, big world out there; this chapter gives you a place to start exploring.

There is more to this book than the printed page. Refer to the *Internet Virtual Worlds Online Companion* page and discover Ventana's online treasure chest. A complete glossary and index are also included.

We'll cover a lot on our quick tour, but don't worry. If you follow along and use your head, you've got nothing to worry about. Let's get going—there's a whole new universe out there.

Sean Carton
February 1995
seancarton@vmedia.com

1

LIFE, DEATH & ADVENTURE ON THE NET

What would you do if you were suddenly given the power to go anywhere or be anyone you wanted? What if it was suddenly possible to enter the worlds of our imagination, worlds filled with exotic peoples, bizarre creatures and fantastic sights, worlds you had only dreamt about?

Today you can. Using only your computer and a connection to the Internet, you have the power at your fingertips to enter thousands of new worlds, places as strange as a distant planet or as familiar and comfortable as a corner coffeehouse. These worlds are not physical places—they're worlds constructed out of words, text-based virtual realties forged from language and the power of the imagination.

The virtual universe is vast and varied. At one moment you could be helping to construct an orbiting space colony at MIT's Cyberion City, and the next you could be frolicking with your animal friends on

FurryMUCK. You can test your mettle in the constant wars on GenocideMUD or just kick back and hang out at Webster's Bar and URL at The Sprawl. If you're the more practical type, you can strap on your virtual backpack and head off to class at Diversity University, the world's first virtual school, or become a contributor to WaxWeb, an ongoing work of collaborative hypermedia. Of course, if all this seems a little too hectic, you can always drop by ZenMOO for a bit of meditation.

All these places are as real and as alive as any city or place you may want to visit in the physical world, but you don't need to find a pile of money, learn a new language or get a bunch of shots before you leave. All you need is a computer, a connection to the Net and a friendly guide (like this one!) to show you the way. What's it like to enter a virtual world? Let's find out...

The World of Virtual Worlds

Your first few minutes could be like this:

You awake naked, defenseless and alone on the cold stone floor of a place that seems to be some sort of temple. Flames shoot up from a pit in the middle of the floor, casting a dim light on the stone walls. You're not sure how you got here, but you know that you need to get moving. You stand up and notice a rough-hewn stone portal to your left. Since there's nowhere else to go, you go through it, out into a cold stone courtyard. Overhead, the sun shines brightly, warming your skin, but reminding you that you need some clothes fast. You glance around the courtyard and notice a small door with a rusting metal sign nailed to it. Looking closer, you can see that the sign reads "Donation Room" in fading letters. This sounds as promising as anything else you've seen so far so you cautiously open the creaking wooden door and step through.

Salvation! The dank floor is strewn with rusted armor and small swords, dented shields and other pieces of equipment. The chill in the room reminds you of your nakedness and you gather up a few items—a cloak, a short sword, a pair of rotted leather sandals, a dented shield—and put them on. You're clothed! You step out of the room and into the courtyard.

Looking around again, feeling flush with good fortune, you notice an archway leading out to a dusty road. You sense that adventure awaits.

As you step into the outside world, you notice a ragtag band of warriors struggling up the hill in front of you. They look tired and battered, bloody from recent battles. You approach one of them.

"Hi! " you say, "What's going on?"

"Not much," one replies, "I got clobbered by the rats in the marsh and I'm headed to the temple to get some rest."

"Oh. I hope things get better," you say, "I'm just starting out. Any hints?"

The warrior grins a tired grin at you and shrugs. "Just stay away from the Sewers until you're at least fifth level. You may want to go north a ways and buy some stuff in town."

"Buy some stuff? But how? I don't have any money?"

"You do now, " he says, "Now I have to be going."

The warrior digs in his bag, and you suddenly find several shiny gold pieces in your hand. You bow thankfully as he trudges off. You stuff the gold into your pockets and look down the road. You can see the gates of a city beckoning you and you begin to realize that there's a lot more here than you thought. Smiling, you shoulder your shield and begin to trudge down the road, ready to take on any adventure that comes your way.

Or your world may read like this:

You're in a closet and you have no idea how you got there. It's pitch dark, and every time you move, you feel small crunchy things under your feet. You grope around wildly, trying to make some sense of where you are, what you're doing here and why you can't seem to turn on the lights. Suddenly, you notice a doorknob. You turn it to open the door and stumble out of the closet into a brightly lit computer room, strewn with coffee cups, printouts and little LEGO pieces.

Definitely not what you expected! As you peer around the room you notice a big Warhol print on the wall, sandwiched in between several bulletin boards, chalkboards and a strange flag. Adding to the happy jumble are several different computer terminals, a stray train transfer ticket and several notes. Not wanting to disturb anything until you know more, you glance around and notice an exit labeled "Center of Centers." That sounds like a good place to start, so you head for the exit.

Still, you haven't bumped into anyone. As you look around, you notice a sign for the Technorhetorician's Bar and Grill. Looks promising! You head over and enter the bar.

You've never seen a bar like this before! In the corner, Godzilla sits at the piano, pounding out tunes on a battered piano. You can hear several animated conversations echo though the room as riotously dressed bar patrons carouse, rolling around in different piles and nervously glancing at Godzilla from time to time. Lou the Bartender, looking pretty hip with his pink Technorhetoricians T-shirt and sporting a stylish pony tail, glances at you as you sit down and decide what to order.

As you mull over your drink selection, you notice that there's a pony sleeping in the corner. Weird, but not too strange. You could get used to this place! You get Lou's attention and order a Pan Galactic Gargle Blaster to sip while you figure out what's going on.

Lou says, "I haven't made one of those in years! I'll have it ready for you in just a minute."

You nod and notice that there are a couple of older gentlemen sitting at the bar with you. You glance at one named Barthes, a silent man sipping Bordeaux. But who is that next to him? It's Derrida, the deconstructionist! What are they doing here? You only have a second to wonder as Barthes turns his head toward you...

Virtual Worlds

You've just experienced what it's like to step into just two of the hundreds of worlds that await you on the Internet. When you enter one of these places, you're stepping into a whole new reality where you can find anything from savage monsters and powerful magic to middle-aged English professors leading discussions on literary theory or people just kicking back and partying. These virtual worlds can be as comfortable and friendly as hanging out at your favorite bar or as terrifying and dangerous as anything you might find in a horror novel. There are games to play, places to mingle, platforms for social research and entire universities where you can take classes. There are nearly as many types of virtual worlds as there are people creating them.

If the whole idea of being able to enter a new world through your computer sounds like science fiction, it's not. Hundreds of virtual worlds exist on the Internet, waiting for you to connect. However, at this point you probably have more than a few questions. Where did these worlds come from and how can you find them? How do you get there and what do you do once you've arrived? Don't worry! You'll find the answers to these and many other questions as we continue through our virtual worlds tour. What once seemed fantastic is now possible.

The Future Is Now

If you've spent any time lately listening to the news, you've heard a lot about the "information superhighway" and how it's going to (someday) bring you video on demand, instant access to information and the ability to connect people all over the world in some sort of vast web of data and communications. You may have heard also about virtual reality and its ability to transport your consciousness into new worlds, sweeping you out of your mundane existence and into fantastic new places. However, you're probably under the impression that all this is around the corner. It's not. It's here. It's now.

Author Gareth Branwyn recently coined the term "datamushroom" to describe the explosion of the Internet. Why datamushroom? Because the Internet—the interconnected web of computers linking people and computers all over the globe—continues to grow and expand every day in ways that no one ever thought possible. It is a cooperative anarchy that functions across national borders and without any central direction, but still manages to function and transmit data worldwide. The neat thing is that because there's no one in charge, people have pretty much been able to do whatever they want, provided certain technical guidelines were met. This has led to the ever-expanding growth of the Net and has given people the freedom to create whatever their minds could envision.

Virtual worlds are some of the most fascinating results of combining the power of the Internet with human creativity. These places don't rely on the rudimentary computer graphics we have available to us today (though this is changing, see Chapter 5), but on the power of our imaginations to take simple descriptions and create entirely new realities. This may not sound like much, but open your favorite novel and see what I mean. Our minds are much better at visualization than computers are.

However, what really sets these new places apart is not just the ability to get online and play a game using words—anyone with a computer can play an adventure game by themselves. Online communities use the power of the Net to bring together people from all over the world into one "place" where they can interact and play and learn together. Bringing people together adds a human element often lacking in our everyday experiences with technology. On top of that, since these places use words to describe everything in them, you can be whoever you want to be. All anyone else will ever know of you is the description that you provide.

Is it live or is it Julia? When you enter a virtual world, you can never be too sure about who you're going to run into—it may be a robot.

Julia is an artificial intelligence program that lives on a computer at Carnegie Mellon. Julia has a habit of logging onto virtual worlds and chatting up a virtual storm with whomever strikes up a conversation. In fact, Julia is so good at what "she" does that she's fooled enough people to take fourth place in the Loebner competition—a test where computer programs are judged on how well they fool a panel of human judges into thinking they're chatting with a human.

Julia used to reside on DruidMUCK but that place seems to be down the last time I checked so Julia's in search of a new home. However, if you want to chat with some silicon, you can still reach Julia by telnetting to julia@fuzine.mt.cs.cmu.edu (yes, that address has an "@" in it) and logging in as julia with no password. If you want to read up on some of her accomplishments, check out Julia's home page on the World Wide Web at http://fuzine.mt.cs.cmu.edu/mlm/julia.html.

Watch out, though, Julia may not be making the rounds any more, but you never know, there may be a Miranda, Betty or Sue...

History of the Virtual World, Part 1

Where did this all begin? Surprisingly enough, it all began back in 1979 at Essex University in the United Kingdom. Roy Trubshaw, an intrepid but bored programmer, got the opportunity to play around with Essex's DEC-10 computer. He wrote a "game" that consisted of a series of connected rooms that allowed people to log on from different terminals to meet and chat. The first version was pretty limited, so he rewrote it. Instead of putting the whole game into one program, it was separated into two parts: a driver program that made things happen, and a database that contained all the room descriptions, all the objects in the rooms and the various commands. Trubshaw christened his new creation MUD, for Multiple User Dungeon. (Actually, the meaning of MUD has been lost in the mists of time, but usually it's been interpreted as Multi-User Domain, Multi-User Dungeon and Multiple User Domain.)

MUD was cool, but it was a bit ahead of its time. Back then, big computers had much less memory and were much slower than most desktop computers today, and the computer at Essex couldn't handle the extra load that MUD put on it. Something had to be done. Richard Bartle, then a student at Essex, re-wrote the game so that it used less processor time and was easier on the computer. What emerged was the precursor to the virtual worlds of today.

With the release of the new version of MUD in the spring of 1980, things began to take off. Around that time, ARPANet (which later became what we know as the Internet), began an experiment with Essex University to link the United Kingdom to the United States. Not long after, MUD got its first user from the outside, when someone from the States logged in to play. Net-based virtual reality was born!

Following MUD, several new online games cropped up, taking their names and themes from popular TV shows (Rock, for Fragile Rock), parodies of Essex University (UNI), and Dungeons and Dragons-type "hack-and-slash" worlds (BLUD). More and more people began to come online to ARPANet and before long, the computers at Essex became swamped with people trying to log on and play MUD. In an effort to spread the word and goad other people into running these games, Richard Bartle sent copies of the MUD program to the United States, Australia, Norway and Sweden—countries that still lead the way in online community development. Eventually, the original MUD was sold to CompuServe, where it still runs under the name of British Legends.

Once the source code (the program that makes the whole thing run) was out, development followed the growth of the Net. Soon, new types of virtual communities began to emerge and, with them, different types of uses were discovered. In 1988 AberMUD (the precursor to most of today's MUDs) was written and passed along to various computers in the United States. From AberMUD came LPMud and DikuMUD, two variants that stressed more of the social aspects of the game while maintaining the old "adventure" aspects. At about the same time, a program called TinyMUD was developed, which allowed players to contribute to the game by way of an internal programming language. TinyMUD led to a whole new class of virtual worlds that emphasized the more social and experimental aspects of virtual interaction. Soon MOO spun off with its own more advanced programming language. MOOs were quickly followed by MUCKs, MUSHes and several other new varieties.

Even though it may seem like a confusing alphabet soup of acronyms at this point, the bottom line is that the virtual worlds family tree has divided into two main branches. On one side are the more "gamelike" virtual worlds, which are usually grouped under the term "MUD." These worlds usually have complicated systems for keeping track of player statistics, battles and quests and the people playing them usually are competing to see who can reach the highest "level." Generally, AberMUD, DikuMUD and LPMud are all referred to as "MUDs."

The other branch of the virtual world tree is a little harder to define, but we can generally group these worlds into the "social" category. In these worlds, you're more likely to find people just hanging out, role playing or using the world as a virtual meeting place. MOO, MUSH, MUCK, TinyMUD and Talkers all generally fall into this category. There's a lot of cross-pollination between the two different trees, but the distinction holds pretty well. Table 1-1 gives a more detailed look at the differences.

Virtual World	Description
MUD	(Multiple User Domain or Multi-User Dungeon) Often used as a generic term for online worlds where many people can connect simultaneously and interact in a shared environment.
AberMUD	One of the earliest types of MUD. AberMUDs lean toward the more traditional hack-and-slash style of playing where the point is to explore, slay monsters and gain experience on the way to attaining higher "levels."
LPMud	Written by Lars Pensjö to correct some of the deficiencies of AberMUD. LPMud's innovation was the introduction of LPC, a language that allowed players to add new areas. Usually, LPMuds are of the hack-and-slash type.
DikuMUD	Developed as an attempt to make MUDding more social. DikuMUD was developed at nearly the same time as LPMud. DikuMUDs are hack-and-slash MUDs with more emphasis on player cooperation.
MOO	(MUD, Object Oriented) One of the more recently developed types of virtual worlds, MOO was first created by Pavel Curtis at the Xerox Palo Alto Research Center. MOOs use a sophisticated programming language that allow people on the MOO to create their own objects and locations. MOOs are almost exclusively social worlds with very little emphasis on game-playing. Some MOOs are being used as teaching and conferencing environments.

MUSH	(Multiple User Shared Hallucination) One of the precursors to MOO, these worlds provide a simple programming language that allows players to create simple objects. MUSHes have a reputation as role-playing worlds, though there are probably as many different themes as there are MUSHes.
MUCK	MUCK doesn't stand for anything—it's a play on the word MUD. MUCKs have internal programming languages like MOOs and MUSHes, and are usually socially oriented.
TinyMUD	The precursor to MOO, MUSH and MUCK, TinyMUD was one of the first virtual world systems to utilize an internal programming language and a play system that stressed player interaction. One of the interesting offshoots of this new interaction was MUD sex, also known as TinySex. Using fast typing and a lascivious imagination, TinySex combines all the interactiveness of phone sex with the flexibility of making yourself look however you want.
Talker	A type of MUD with little or no emphasis put on creating a virtual environment. Mainly, Talkers are places for people to meet and chat. Generally most Talkers are modified versions of other MUD systems that have few if any "locations."

Table 1-1: *Description of the many different virtual worlds.*

Today, intrepid hackers continue developing new virtual worlds. Some of the more recent experiments involve interfacing MUDs with the World Wide Web, adding graphics to MUDs and using virtual worlds to research how people interact and create in new environments. Besides gaming, people are using the MUDs to hold classes, meet other people, have online meetings, and create and display art. People are discovering the limitless possibilities when people are brought together in a virtual world.

Maybe that's the reason why virtual worlds continue to become more popular. In a world where technology often seems to separate people, MUDs bring people together in ways that were never possible before. After all, it's the human element that keeps things interesting!

Moving On

As you've seen, the virtual worlds of the Internet are much more than games. Some are games, but others are research centers, experiments in virtual reality, meeting places and even schools. Each virtual world is unique.

Not all virtual world systems are equal. There are generally about eight major types of virtual world systems or program types, and these systems can be divided into two separate classes: game-oriented MUDs and socially oriented virtual worlds. However, there's a lot of cross-breeding between the two classes, so you can't always rely on the type of system when you're trying to classify them.

By now you're probably itching to get started. Before we embark, however, we'll need to spend a little time deciding how we're going to get there, what mode of travel we'll use and how we'll get the supplies we'll need to help us on our journeys. In Chapter 2 we'll try to solve these problems. We'll delve into what kind of Internet connection to get, what types of programs we'll need to connect to the different virtual worlds and how to download these programs from the Internet. So, sit back and follow along as we outfit ourselves and get ready to log on.

2

GETTING CONNECTED

Until I logged onto a virtual world for the first time, I really thought that the Internet was just a big post office and software library. I knew that by clicking an icon, I could get a nice menu that let me read my e-mail and download software—but that was about as far as my Net knowledge went. Then, one day, I read an article about the MIT Media Lab that mentioned an online world called the "MediaMOO" that let you log on, talk to other people and create stuff. Well, for someone who thought that the Internet was just a quick way to contact my friends, this was quite a revelation! I had to check it out.

The article mentioned an address that you needed to connect to the MediaMOO. I knew a little bit about addresses from my e-mail excursions and I figured (correctly) that using the address in the article would allow me to connect to the MediaMOO. However, I had no idea how to use this address.

I spent the next few days vainly searching for a way to hook up. I looked for a place in my e-mail program that would let me connect. No dice. I tried connecting with the program I used for transferring files.

Again, nothing, though I did get some pretty interesting error messages. Finally, I walked over to the computer lab and bared my soul. "How do, um, I, um, use this address to, uh, connect to this place?" I asked, sheepishly pointing to where I had scrawled the MediaMOO's Internet address on a piece of paper. A man looked up from the printout he was studying and said the word that opened the doors to the online universe: "telnet."

To make a long story short, after a few minutes of chatting I learned how to use a program called "telnet" to connect to the MediaMOO and I was off surfing the Net! With one six-letter UNIX command, a whole new universe opened for me.

The moral of this story is that we all have to start somewhere. Getting an Internet account and learning how to use even the most basic functions can be a pretty daunting task, and nobody, no matter how Net-savvy they appear to be, is born with the knowledge of how to use the Internet.

I'm not going to try to teach you everything about the Internet (there are plenty of good books on that subject, see the sidebar for some suggestions) and I'm assuming you at least know what the Internet is, but there are a few issues that we'll need to cover before you head out into the online world. We'll look at how you can connect to the Net, what software you'll need once you're there and how to use that software to connect to a virtual world.

How do I find out more about the Net? If you are new to the Internet or just want to learn more about what's out there, there are several books and free guides you can check out.

- The *Internet Tour Guide* series (Ventana Press, 1995.) Written for both the Macintosh and Windows platforms, these books are great introductions for novice Net-heads. They come with several companion disks full of useful software that will have you surfing the Net in no time.
- *Zen and the Art of the Internet by Brendan Kehoe*. This venerable guide to the Internet is available both online and in book form. If you have an America Online account, you can find the entire document indexed in the Internet Connections section. If you know how to use anonymous ftp, you can find it at the Electronic Frontier Foundation's site ftp.eff.org or at csi.jpl.nasa.gov. If you want to find out about how to use ftp, read on in this chapter.
- *The Big Dummy's Guide to the Internet* by Adam Gaffin. This is another guide that you can find at the Electronic Frontier Foundation's site at ftp.eff.org. It's one of the best beginner's "Net in a nutshell" guides available. It's also available from the EFF's file library on America Online.

Necessary Connections

First, let's back up a bit and define the Internet. What makes the Internet the Internet? It all boils down to this: the Net is a bunch of computers connected together all speaking to each other with a common language called TCP/IP. Because all these computers speak to each other with a common language, all computers that connect to the Internet use their own versions of this common language to interact with each other. The beauty of this system is that even though there may be hundreds (if not thousands) of different brands of computers connected to the Internet, as long as they speak to each other the same way, they all get along.

Note: There's a lot of terminology we'll have to cover in this chapter, and you'll have enough to absorb without getting bogged down in semantic arguments. So, for the sake of clarity, in this chapter I'm going to refer to all virtual worlds as "MUDs." We'll worry about the distinctions later.

To connect to a virtual world on the Internet, you have to be connected to the Internet. Let's examine some of the ways that you can log on.

Shell Accounts

There are three ways for you to connect to the Internet. The first, and most common way, is called a shell account. With this type of account you sit at home and connect to a host computer using your modem and communications software. When you dial in and log onto your account, you're given space in the host to store information as well as access to programs that allow you to access other computers and computer resources on the Internet. Because you are dialing in and remotely accessing the host's capabilities, you can only use programs that run on the host. These programs are almost exclusively text-based—when you get a menu or are asked a question or want to run a program, you do so by typing keyboard commands to the host computer.

Direct Connections

The second method of connecting to the Net is to make your computer an actual Internet-connected computer. When you want to do something on the Net, you run programs to do what you want on your computer, not on a host.

The ultimate way of doing this is through a direct Net connection. By directly connecting your computer to the Net through a dedicated line leased from the phone company, you get blazing speed and nearly instantaneous access to most Internet resources. Unfortunately this method is so expensive that only large organizations with big budgets can afford the most high-speed connections.

SLIP/PPP Accounts

There is a compromise. The level of connection between a host account and a direct connection is called a SLIP or PPP account. With one of these babies, you dial up a host using special software. When you connect, the host actually gives you your own temporary Internet connection through the phone line. You're on the Net! This method allows you all the advantages of a direct Net connection and the economy of a shell account. The only drawback is that it's a little slow, but it's usually fine for home purposes. We can just consider a SLIP/PPP account to be a slow-speed direct connection.

Either way you decide to connect, you need to do so through an Internet service provider. To find one, send the message **PDIAL** to info-deli-server@netcom.com. You'll get back Peter Kaminski's PDIAL list of all Internet service providers. Of course, this does present a bit of a Catch-22 to all of you who don't have Net access. Try having a friend on the Net download it for you or try checking the phone book for a service provider near you.

University Accounts

If you're a student at a large college or university, chances are you already have an Internet account waiting for you. Jog on over to your campus computer center and find out how you can get logged on.

Type of Account	Pros	Cons
Shell Account	Least expensive way to connect to the Net Easy to connect No complicated software Reliable Simple to set up and maintain Often free to university students and people from government agencies	Limited to software that will run on host Have to learn UNIX or VMS operating system Cannot use graphical interface Downloading needs to be done twice—first to host, then to home Disk quotas—you only have limited space on the host to store your files
Direct Connection	You can use familiar software on your own computer Access to graphical World Wide Web browsers FTP straight to your computer No disk quotas: you store everything on your own computer	More complicated to set up Often more expensive Can be less reliable than a shell account Can sometimes be slower to use for things like e-mail and USENET News

Table 2-1: *Shell versus Direct Internet connections.*

Telnet: Gateway to the Virtual Universe

Once you've gotten the details of how you're going to connect to the Internet ironed out, you're going to need some way to connect to a MUD. If you recall my story from the beginning of the chapter, you'll remember that I first learned how to connect to MUDs using something called "telnet." Let's look at how to use telnet.

Each computer on the Internet is identified by unique name and number. This name is referred to as a *domain name*. Each domain name also has a corresponding numeric *domain address*. A computer's address is just like your street address—it's unique to that computer and no other. Once you know the address of a MUD, you use telnet to connect to that MUD by giving it the address and port number of the MUD you're trying to connect to. Telnet then does its job, leaping across the Net and connecting you to the MUD.

Banning MUDding If you use a university account to access the Internet, check with your systems administrator or check the rules that the school posts about the computer system. Many schools are starting to ban MUDding among students for two reasons. One, MUDding eats up computer resources that students need for "legitimate" work. Second, MUD-addiction can become a serious problem. There are many stories floating around the Net about students who flunked out of school or lost their jobs because they didn't spend enough time in real life to take care of their obligations.

If your school has configured its systems so that you can't connect to a MUD, they've probably done so by blocking your ability to telnet to different access ports used by MUDs. You really can't get around this, and I suggest that you don't even try. Some system administrators can be pretty cranky if they find out that someone has been trying to hack the system to play MUDs. Besides, if you're that advanced, you probably wouldn't be reading this book anyway!

Just remember: it's only a game. If you're using a university, government or business connection to the Net, MUDding is a privilege, not a right.

Telnet With a Shell Account

Since telnet is a program, it may look different to you depending on just what kind of Internet connection you have.

To use telnet on a shell account, you have to tell the computer that you want to use telnet, and where you want to connect to. For example, if you wanted to connect to a MUD located at cyberspace.com 4000, you'd type the following at your UNIX shell prompt:

telnet cyberspace.com 4000

If you're using a VMS system, you'd probably have to type something like this:

telnet cyberspace.com/port=4000

Let's dissect what you just typed. First, the command **telnet** tells the host computer that you are going to be using its telnet program to jaunt out across the Net. Next, **cyberspace.com** is the domain name of the computer. The "com" in the name refers to the fact that this machine is a "commercial" one, run by a business and not a university or government site. Finally, the **4000** is the "port number." Each machine on the Net accepts input from many different sources, and each source has its own "port" that allows that information in. In this case, the port numbered 4000 has been set aside for MUD connections.

Once you type this command and press Enter (or Return), telnet leaps out across the Net and connects you to the virtual world located at the address that you entered (see Chapter 3 to find out what happens once you connect). From that point on, everything you type goes directly to the remote computer rather than the host you are using. Once you disconnect from the MUD, you'll be returned to your host computer. Pretty simple, huh?

Telnet With a Direct Connection

Those of you with SLIP/PPP connections may be wondering how telnet applies to you since you aren't typing commands into a host. Telnet is just a program that runs on the host computer to connect you to other computers. If you are on the Net through a SLIP/PPP connection, *you* are the host computer so you'll have to run a telnet program for your machine.

Probably the two most popular telnet programs for personal computers are NCSA Telnet for the Macintosh and Trumpet Telnet for PC compatibles. NCSA Telnet for the Macintosh is available from anonymous ftp in the ncsa.uiuc.edu/Telnet/Mac/ directory. If you need help with anonymous ftp, check out the section on page 29–31, which covers downloading a MUD client. Trumpet Telnet is part of the winapps2.zip archive, which can be found at ftp.halcyon.com in the pub/slip/winsock directory. If you don't know how to use ftp to get these files, just jump ahead to page 29 to get a detailed introduction to ftp.

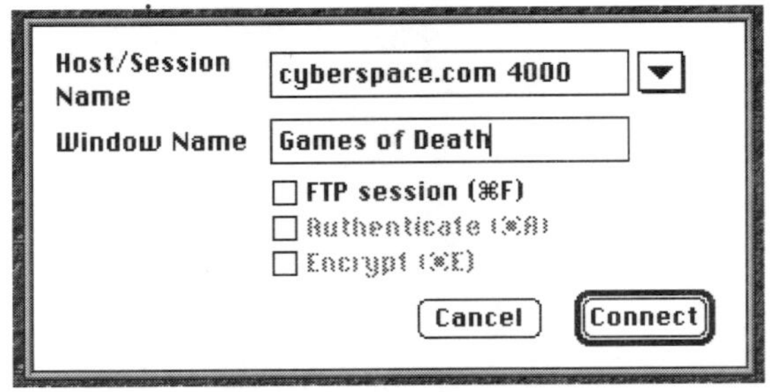

Figure 2-1: *NCSA telnet connection dialog box.*

Using Telnet With a Mac

To connect with NCSA Telnet for the Mac,

1. Make sure your SLIP/PPP connection is established and you have the NCSA Telnet program installed on your computer.
2. Click the NCSA Telnet program icon to begin the program. The opening screen and the menu bar appears.
3. To open a connection to the Games Of Death MUD, select Open Connection from the File menu. The Connect dialog box appears, as shown in Figure 2-1.
4. Type **mud.cyberspace.com 4000** in the Host/Session Name field and **Games of Death** in the Window Name field, then click the Connect button.
5. Telnet now attempts to connect to the MUD. Once a connection is made, a window containing your connection appears (see Figure 2-2).

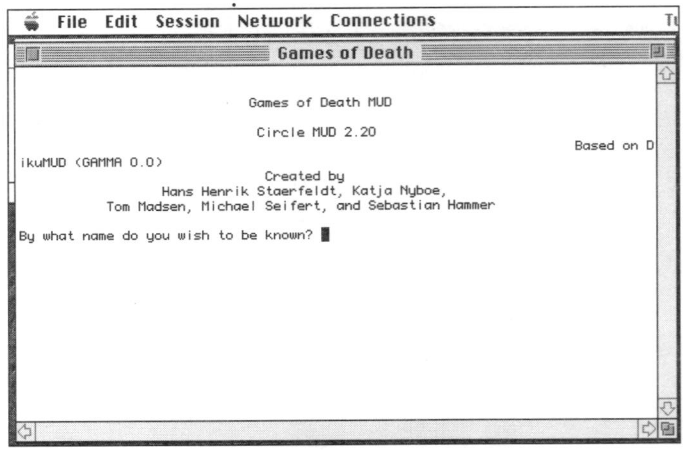

Figure 2-2: *Connected using NCSA telnet.*

6. You're connected! If you want to start your MUDding, jump ahead to Chapter 3. If you're not ready yet, disconnect by choosing Close from the File menu.

If you want to connect to the same world again, you can do so quickly and easily by saving a *set*. A telnet set contains all the information the computer needs to get you back to that MUD. Before you disconnect from the MUD, select Save Set from the File menu. Give the saved set the same name as the MUD you've connected to. Later, when you want to zip back to play that MUD, just run NCSA Telnet and select Load Set from the File menu. You'll be back in a flash!

Store all your MUD telnet sets in a folder by themselves. When you want to play, make sure your SLIP/PPP connection is up and then all you have to do is double-click that MUD's icon to be there instantly.

Using Telnet With a PC

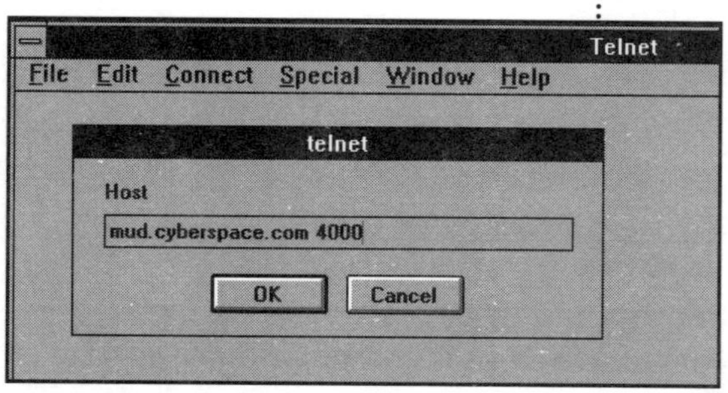

Figure 2-3: *Entering an address in Trumpet Telnet.*

If you're using Trumpet Telnet on your PC, the procedure is pretty much the same.

1. Start Trumpet Telnet from the Windows Program Manager.
2. When you start Trumpet Telnet, a Host dialog box appears. Enter the address you are telnetting to, followed by a colon and the port number. For example, if you wanted to telnet to cyberspace.com 4000, you'd enter **mud.cyberspace.com:4000** in the Host dialog box. See Figure 2-3.
3. Click the OK button to connect and you're off!

Clients: Telnet With an Attitude

Now that you've seen how to use telnet, it's time to face facts: telnet is a boring way to log on. Telnet does one thing and it does it well, but it doesn't provide any extra features to make your life online any easier.

Clients jazz things up a bit. Like telnet, a client lets you take off across the Net and contact other computers. In addition, clients provide all sorts of features that make your MUD life easier. First, most MUD clients allow you to split your screen so that incoming text from the MUD is in one screen and the stuff that you type is in another. This feature gets really useful during chat sessions where you are in a room with a bunch of other people all talking at once. Also, clients can do stuff like gagging (turning off text other people write), word wrapping, highlighting text and even auto-login so that you never have to type your name and password again. As you get more advanced in your MUDding, clients even let you set up macros to define new commands, triggers that automatically reply to actions on the MUD and aliases that allow you to change MUD commands into words that are easier and quicker to type. Table 2-2 provides a brief glossary of some of the more popular MUD client features.

Word	Feature
Aliases	Allows you to shorten a long command. Some commands are pretty common and you'll find yourself typing them over and over again. When you alias a command, you change its name into something easier to type. For example, whenever you kill a monster, you may normally have to type **Get all from corpse** to get all the monster's loot. Aliases let you substitute gac for that long phrase, so if you want to get all, just type **gac**.
Auto-login	Automatically connects you to the MUD with your pre-set name and password. This capability becomes really useful when you start to play many different MUDs and don't want to have to remember a different password for each.

Gagging	Lets you "gag" certain other players so that anything they display won't be visible on your screen. Useful if you find yourself pestered by an annoying character.
Highlighting	Highlights or emphasizes certain words or groups of words so that they stand out from the rest of the text scrolling up your screen. When you turn on this feature, you must specify what you want highlighted.
Logging	Captures all the stuff on your screen into a text file that you can read later. Useful if you want to relive past glory or want to have time off-line to mull over a particularly hard puzzle.
Macros	Reduces a series of commands that you normally have to type in their entirety to a single keystroke. Save those fingers for those marathon chat sessions!
Mapping	Assists you in mapping new terrain. Not a really common feature.
Multiple Login	Lets you to maintain multiple connections to a MUD, allowing you to play two or more characters at once. Many MUDs frown on this practice, but some people do it anyway.
Split Screen	Splits the screen into two different areas—one area that displays stuff coming in from the MUD, and one area that just shows what you type. Helps eliminate the confusion of mixed-up text when MUD activity gets hot and heavy.
Triggers	Lets you establish and define predetermined responses to actions on the MUD. The client "looks" for certain MUD actions and then sends your canned response.
Word Wrapping	Wraps text where it should be—in the spaces between the words. Most telnet programs are pretty lame when it comes to handling text. Since a lot of MUDs (and particularly MOOs) send text as one long string, telnet usually just breaks words when they reach the edge of the screen, not keeping them together like we're used to.

Table 2-2: *Glossary of popular MUD client features.*

Using a client can make your MUDding life a heck of a lot easier, but all the extra functions can steepen the learning curve a bit. If you're a beginner (which I'm assuming you are), you'd probably be better off just sticking to telnet in the beginning. However, as you get more experience online, you'll find a client helpful. Let's take a brief look at getting a client and setting it up.

Getting & Setting Up a Client

First, you need to get a MUD client. Which one you get depends on your Internet connection. If you are using a dial-up or shell account, chances are that the host your account resides on uses UNIX or VMS as its operating system. If so, check with your systems administrator to find out if someone has already installed a MUD client for your use. If you use a pay provider (as opposed to a "free" school account), they probably have one installed. Check your documentation or ask your systems administrator or tech support person.

If you don't have a client installed on your system and you use a dial-up account, you'll have to install one yourself. Because there are so many different types of computers out there, most clients are distributed as source code, e.g., the actual program code that you compile on your host machine. This isn't a task for the easily frightened. Some clients will compile quite nicely, but some might need a little tweaking to get them to work correctly on your machine. Unless you have some knowledge of computer programming, it's best to read the documentation very carefully and then find some computer guru to help you out.

The next step is to decide what client you want to use. There are many clients out there, some good, some bad, some ugly, but all with a plethora of features. Let's take a look at some of the more popular MUD clients and see what they've got.

Popular MUD Clients

Most clients offer the basic functions of word wrapping, split-screen displays, and various macro and alias capabilities. The biggest differences are what kind of system the client runs on and how easy it is to use. You'll have to decide the ease-of-use question yourself, but as for the connection detail, generally there are two types: shell account clients that run under UNIX or VMS, and direct-connection clients that run on Macintosh or PC-compatible personal computers. You need to select which type of client to use based on what kind of connection you have. Below are listed some of the most popular clients.

The Virtual Worlds Quick Tour Online Companion Ventana offers an *Online Companion* for the *Virtual Worlds Quick Tour* as part of the Ventana Visitor's Center. The *Online Companion* includes all the software mentioned in the *Quick Tour*, with the latest versions accessible as soon as they are made available, along with version change notes; Chapter 8, the online virtual world listings; and the Internet Meta-MUD, the MUD of MUDs, Ventana's virtual world. There is also an online guide that will provide you with quick access to Internet resources related to this book. The *Virtual Worlds Quick Tour Online Companion* will help make this book dynamic, up-to-date and continually useful.

The *Online Companion* can be found at http://www. vmedia.com/ivwqt.html

UNIX Clients

UNIX client programs require the UNIX operating system to run. If you have a shell account, chances are that you are using UNIX. Even though there are several different versions of UNIX in use today—System V, BSD, IRIX, Ultrix, etc.—most UNIX MUD client programs are generic enough to run on just about any flavor of UNIX. Read the documentation that comes with the client to find out the details about installing it on your shell account.

Tiny Fugue

Also known by its UNIX command name, tf, Tiny Fugue's features are primarily geared toward Tiny MUDs but it also provides a simple-to-use interface for Diku- and LPMuds. Tiny Fugue allows you great flexibility in defining your highlights and gags, as well as supporting auto-login, word wrapping and split-screen entry, along with capabilities for defining macros and triggers. The word on the Net is that this is one of the easiest clients to learn to use. Check it out. Figure 2-4 shows what it looks like in action.

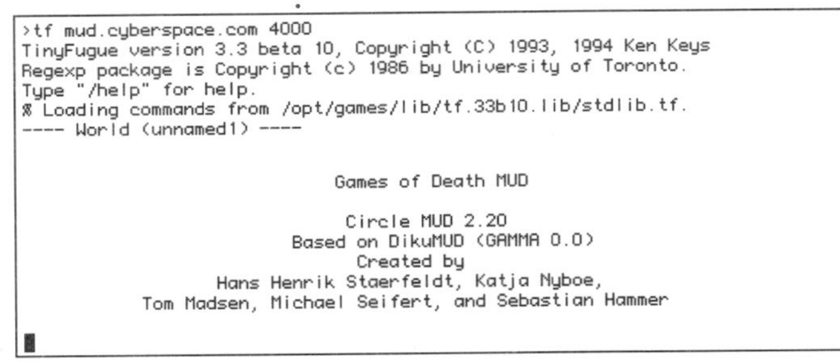

Figure 2-4: *Tiny Fugue.*

TinTin & TinTin++

TinTin, the original of the pair, is a client designed for use with DikuMUDs, but you'll probably find its features useful for other worlds you might visit along the way. Running under UNIX, TinTin includes such features as triggers, macros and multiple connections. TinTin++, the successor to TinTin, adds split-screen entry. Figure 2-5 shows TinTin++ being used.

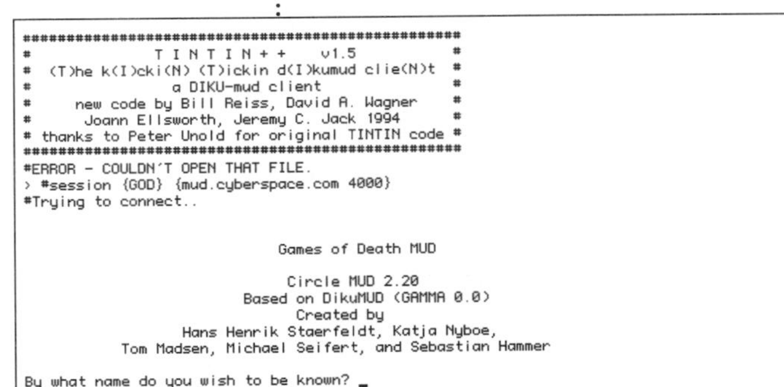

Figure 2-5: *TinTin++.*

TinyTalk

This is one of the most popular UNIX MUD clients, running under both BSD and System V UNIX. TinyTalk includes almost all the most popular features: logging, highlighting, gagging, auto-login and macros. Additionally, TinyTalk supports cyberportals—a MUD feature that connects you to other MUDs. TinyTalk is designed to work best with Tiny MUDs.

VMS & Emacs Clients

I've lumped these two together not because they share a common operating system, but because they make up the minority of MUD clients. VMS is an operating system used by VAX computers. You probably won't find a commercial Internet service provider uses VMS for its users' shell accounts, but if you have an account on a university or business computer, there's a good chance you might be on a VAX. Check with your systems administrator if you're not sure. Emacs isn't an operating system but an extremely powerful programmable editor that runs on a variety of systems.

TINT

For those of you on VAX machines (or any other hosts that happen to be running under VMS), TINT is a popular alternative to UNIX-based clients. Besides the usual host of nifty features—highlighting, screen modes, macros—TINT also provides support for file uploading, a useful feature if you need to shovel lots of text upline all at once.

MUD.el

Not for the faint of heart, MUD.el is a LISP-programmed extension to the superpowerhouse editor Emacs. MUD.el provides just about all the usual client extras with highlighting, macros, logging and split-screen mode standard. Also, unlike many MUD clients, MUD.el isn't really too picky about what kind of MUD you want to use it with. Because it runs under Emacs, it can take advantage of most of this powerful editor's features, but you have to brave a pretty steep learning curve before you'll learn all of its features.

Personal Computer Clients: Macintosh & Windows

Generally, most personal computer clients are designed to be used with a direct Net connection. The advantage of using a client that's designed to run on your desktop computer through a direct Net connection is that most clients use graphical user interfaces to make your MUDding smoother.

VWMud

VWMud is a fairly popular MUD client for Windows written by a fellow named Vaughn Wynne-Jones, a Dallas, Texas-based journalist. This client is heavily oriented toward making your MUD battles easier, and sports nifty features like user-definable triggers and macros. The VWMud client also takes advantage of the graphic capabilities of Windows by displaying your character's health and status in several "status bars" and by allowing you to use movement buttons rather than commands to move through the MUD. Its only drawback is that you must know the numeric IP address for any MUD that you want to contact because VWMud can't handle text names. Figure 2-6 shows VWMud at work.

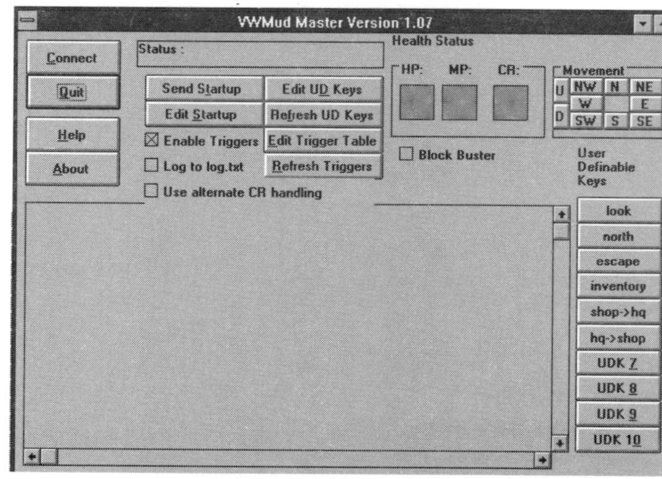

Figure 2-6: *VWMud at work.*

MUDDweller

This is perhaps the most popular of the two Mac MUD clients, mainly because of its sheer simplicity and ease of use—just enter the IP address and port of the MUD you want to reach, select Connect and bingo! You're there in a jiffy. MUDDweller features a split-screen interface, triggers, macros and multiple

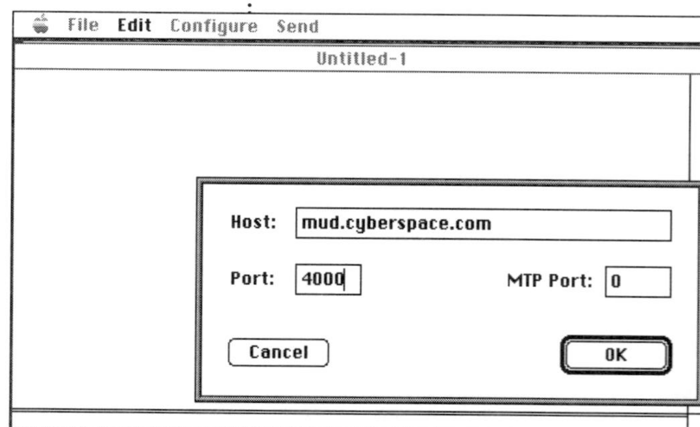

Figure 2-7: *Using MUDDweller to connect to a MUD.*

connections. You can save your configuration sets for each MUD you play, making calling back as easy as double-clicking an icon. MUDDweller will work over a SLIP/PPP connection, as well as a regular dial-up account. Look at Figure 2-7 to see what MUDDweller looks like.

Mudling

Larger and more sophisticated than MUDDweller, Mudling provides macros, split screens, triggers and aliases among its helpful features. Mudling also includes a very interesting feature not often found in MUD clients—it makes a map for you as you explore! (See Figure 2-8.) By using a special "map mode" and movement keys, Mudling draws a map of your path as you travel, even giving you the option of printing the map for later use. This feature is still in its developmental stages and doesn't seem to fare too well with complex terrain. Even so, it is a great start!

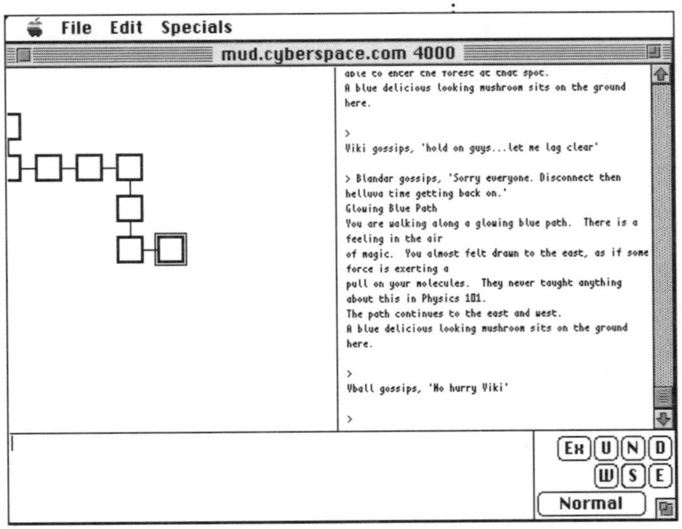

Figure 2-8: *Mudling in Map mode.*

Getting the Goods: Using FTP

Now that you know what clients are out there, how do you get one? You need to use another program called File Transfer Protocol (ftp) that allows you to go to different computers on the Internet and download software. Let's take a look at how to use ftp.

Downloading with ftp isn't all that different than using telnet. First you must connect with the ftp site. Table 2-3 lists the site names and ftp addresses for a number of MUD client ftp sites. To standardize things, the client ftp sites are identified using URLs (Uniform Resource Locators). The first "ftp://" means that you want to ftp. Following that is the Net address of the ftp server. Following the address is the path to the client directory. A path is the series of directories you have to go through in order to get to what you are looking for.

Client	Site
Oklahoma State University MUD site	ftp://ftp.math.okstate.edu/pub/muds/clients/
Xerox Parc	ftp://parcftp.xerox.com/pub/MOO/clients
The Comnet Project	ftp://ftp.tcp.com/pub/mud/Clients
University of Toronto	ftp://ftp.white.toronto.edu/pub/muds/tcltt
Lysator University	ftp://ftp.lysator.liu.se/pub/lpmud/clients
Princeton University	ftp://ftp.princeton.edu/pub/tintin++/dist
The Institute for Information & Media Science	ftp://imv.aau.dk/pub/Mudling
University of California: Oakland	ftp://oak.oakland.edu/pub/msdos/pktdrvr
Ventana Media	ftp://ftp.vmedia.com/pub/windows/mud

Table 2-3: *MUD Client ftp sites.*

FTPing With a Shell Account

If you're using a shell account to access the Internet,

```
>ftp oak.oakland.edu
Connected to oak.oakland.edu.
220 oak.oakland.edu FTP server (Version wu-2.4(8) Wed Jan 18 20:05:05 EST 1995)
ready.
Name (oak.oakland.edu:elrod): anonymous
331 Guest login ok, send your complete e-mail address as password.
Password:
230-
230-                          Welcome to
230-                   THE OAK SOFTWARE REPOSITORY
230-          A service of Oakland University, Rochester Michigan
230-
230- If you have trouble using OAK with your ftp client, please try using
230- a dash (-) as the first character of your password -- this will turn
230- off the continuation messages that may be confusing your ftp client.
230- OAK is a Unix machine, and filenames are case sensitive.
230-
230- Access is allowed at any time.  If you have any unusual problems,
230- please report them via electronic mail to archives@Oakland.Edu
230-
230- You are user #180 out of 400 maximum users on Tue Feb  7 19:52:01 1995.
230-
230- Oak is also on the World Wide Web, URL: http://www.acs.oakland.edu/oak.html
```

Figure 2-9: *Logging into an ftp server.*

```
ftp> ls -la
200 PORT command successful.
150 Opening ASCII mode data connection for /bin/ls.
total 3382
drwxr-xr-x   2 w8sdz    OAK         8192 Feb  5 16:29 .
drwxr-xr-x 218 w8sdz    OAK         8192 Feb  7 01:28 ..
-rw-r--r--   1 w8sdz    OAK         2534 Feb  5 16:27 00_index.txt
-rw-r--r--   1 w8sdz    OAK         3486 Feb  4 19:34 00_pktdr.zip
-rw-r--r--   1 w8sdz    OAK        32264 Dec 11  1992 dis_pkt9.zip
-rw-r--r--   1 w8sdz    OAK        86128 Jun  6  1994 exp16116.zip
-rw-r--r--   1 w8sdz    OAK        26703 Jun 18  1992 ipxtcpip.zip
-rw-r--r--   1 w8sdz    OAK        78214 Oct 19  1993 mudcal23.zip
-rw-r--r--   1 w8sdz    OAK        26173 Apr  2  1992 novell.zip
-rw-r--r--   1 w8sdz    OAK       197182 May 30  1993 pcg3.zip
-rw-r--r--   1 w8sdz    OAK       381383 Jan 13  1990 pcip_pkt.zip
-rw-r--r--   1 w8sdz    OAK        29000 Apr  2  1992 pdether.zip
-rw-r--r--   1 w8sdz    OAK        15323 Sep 29  1992 pdipx103.zip
-rw-r--r--   1 w8sdz    OAK       118654 Apr 10  1994 pdtst217.zip
-rw-r--r--   1 w8sdz    OAK       435420 Nov 23  1993 pktd11.zip
-rw-r--r--   1 w8sdz    OAK       326152 Nov 23  1993 pktd11a.zip
-rw-r--r--   1 w8sdz    OAK       344847 Nov 23  1993 pktd11b.zip
```

Figure 2-10: *Ftp directory listing.*

1. First, type **ftp** followed by the address of the ftp server (e.g., **oak.oakland.edu**) and press Enter (or Return). It should look similar to Figure 2-9.
2. At the Name prompt, type a**nonymous** and press Enter (or Return).
3. You should then get a password prompt. Type your e-mail address and then enter:

   331 Guest login ok, send your complete e-mail address as password.
   Password:

4. After you type your password you'll see the greeting screen and then a prompt. To get to the clients directory, you need to change directories. To do that, type **cd** and then the path to the directory (the path follows the site name in the listings). In this case, type the following:

   ftp> cd pub/msdos/pktdrvr

you should then see this:

   250 CWD command successful.
   ftp>

5. Now you're in the right directory. To get a listing of files, type **/s-/a** and press Enter (or Return). You should see a listing similar to Figure 2-10.

The file that we want to get is called mudcal23.zip. You can see it on the right side of the file listing in Figure 2-10. If your file listing looks a little different, don't worry—as long as you can see the name of the files you'll be OK.

Now to get the file. First, since .zip files are in binary format, you must set your type to binary. Type **bin** and press Enter (or Return). Next, to get the file just type **get** and then the file name. See Figure 2-11.

```
ftp> bin
200 Type set to I.
ftp> get mudcal23.zip
200 PORT command successful.
150 Opening BINARY mode data connection for mudcal23.zip (78214 bytes).
226 Transfer complete.
local: mudcal23.zip remote: mudcal23.zip
78214 bytes received in 10 seconds (7.6 Kbytes/s)
ftp> █
```

Figure 2-11: *Transferring a file with ftp.*

You're done! The file is now in your account on your host computer. Type **bye** to exit ftp. Check with your system administrator on how to download files from your host to your home computer.

Using a SLIP/PPP Account

If you're using a SLIP/PPP account there are many other ftp programs available such as Anarchie or Fetch for the Macintosh or WinFTP for Windows. Check the documentation on that particular client that you intend to use. The commands are basically the same, though: connect to the server, change directories and get the file you want.

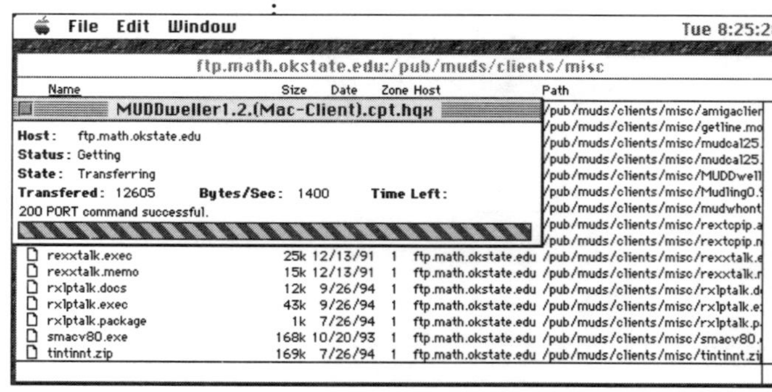

Figure 2-12: *Using Anarchie to snag a file.*

Using a World Wide Web Browser

You can also use a World Wide Web browser to download a client. Select the option to open a URL and type in the entire URL that you see in the client ftp list. You should then get a listing of all the files in that directory. Select the one you want and watch it download! See Figure 2-13.

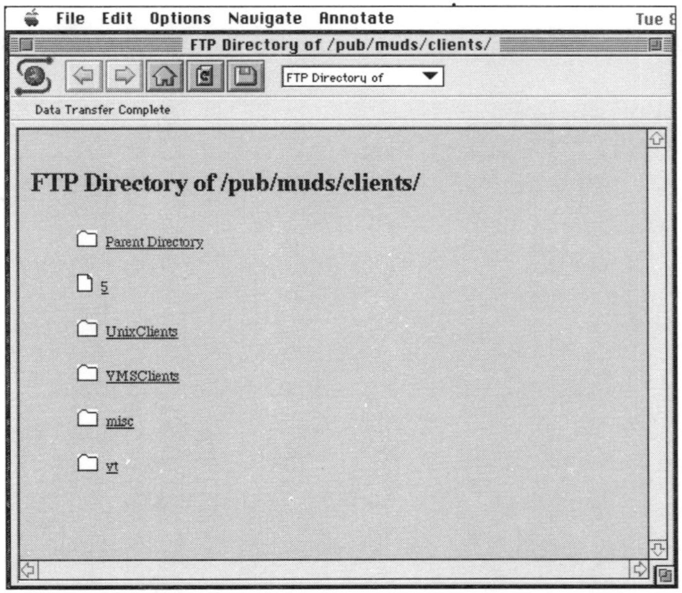

Figure 2-13: *Using the NCSA Mosaic WWW browser to ftp a file.*

Moving On

Now that you've learned the basics of how to connect to virtual worlds using telnet and client programs you're probably itching to head off into the virtual universe. Wait no longer! In Chapter 3 we'll use telnet to log onto a MUD for the first time. Once we're there, we'll create your first character, learn some basic movement and communication skills, and find out what you need to know to survive. Who knows, we may even run into some serious adventures along the way. So, go brew a pot of coffee, put that cat out for the night, lock your door and prepare to get in the game!

3

GETTING IN THE GAME

Once you've decided how you're going to connect to a MUD, either through telnet from your shell or direct account, or by using a MUD client, it's time to jack into your first MUD! For your first MUD adventure, let's go to the Games of Death MUD, a fairly standard DikuMUD. Though there are hundreds of different MUDs on the Internet, the procedures we'll cover here are fairly similar. If you follow along through this example, you'll be more than prepared when you decide to spread your wings and head off to new MUDs.

As we go on our first virtual journey, it's important to remember a few things. First, the online world is always changing. That's what makes it so exciting. However, that also means that as we go along, things may not look exactly the same as they do in the book. Don't panic! Even if things look different, the same concepts apply. Try to read ahead and use the concepts in this book to figure out what to do. Remember—you're an explorer! Expect the unexpected.

Even though our first journey will take us to a DikuMUD, the commands you learn on our trip don't apply to just one type of MUD. In fact, I've tried to stick close to the basics. On other MUDs, these basic commands will almost certainly be exactly the same or very similar to what you've learned. The most important command—the help command— is the same everywhere you go. Learn how to use it.

Making the Connection

First, make sure you are logged onto your account. (See Chapter 2, "Getting Connected," for more information about getting connected.) Next, you need to tell telnet or your client program where you want to go. If you're using a shell account, type:

telnet mud.cyberspace.com 4000

If you're using a MUD client or a direct connection version of telnet running on your own machine, this procedure may be a little different. Check your documentation to get the exact syntax, but basically, all you're doing is telling the program where you want to connect to.

HOT TIP

If you ever try telnetting to a MUD and get a 'login:' prompt instead of something that looks like a MUD, you've probably forgotten to enter the port number. If you do this, the computer thinks you're trying to enter its normal user area. Just press Enter until it logs you off and then check to make sure you've entered the correct number.

Now, sit back as you zip off across the Net. You probably won't see anything for a few seconds but, if all goes all right, you'll see the Games of Death logon screen, which looks something like Figure 3-1.

```
>telnet mud.cyberspace.com 4000
Trying 199.2.48.50 ...
Connected to mud.cyberspace.com.
Escape character is '^]'.

                    Games of Death MUD

                      Circle MUD 2.20
                 Based on DikuMUD (GAMMA 0.0)
                         Created by
            Hans Henrik Staerfeldt, Katja Nyboe,
      Tom Madsen, Michael Seifert, and Sebastian Hammer

By what name do you wish to be known? _
```

Figure 3-1: *Connecting to the Games of Death MUD.*

Congratulations! You've connected to your first MUD! What's all this stuff mean? First, the top few lines are not generated by Games of Death, but by your host computer as it tries to connect to the MUD using telnet. The numbers you see—"Trying 199.2.48.50..."—represent the IP number of the computer you're trying to telnet to. This number means basically the same thing as the name "mud.cyberspace.com" but since computers are way dumber than people, they really don't understand word names. You host computer's domain-name server knows that cyberspace.com really equals 199.2.48.50 on the Internet, saving you the trouble of having to know the hard-to-remember numeric address by substituting the number for the name when you telnet.

The next few lines:

> **Connected to mud.cyberspace.com.**
> **Escape character is '^]'.**

appear when telnet has successfully established a connection. You might notice that it says mud.cyberspace.com. The next few lines tell you that you've reached the Games of Death MUD.

```
                    Games of Death MUD

                      Circle MUD 2.20
                 Based on DikuMUD (GAMMA 0.0)
                         Created by
            Hans Henrik Staerfeldt, Katja Nyboe,
      Tom Madsen, Michael Seifert, and Sebastian Hammer

   By what name do you wish to be known? _
```

Figure 3-2: *Games of Death logon screen.*

Figure 3-2 shows the logon screen. Most MUDs have one, some fancier and some plainer. This is the doorway to the MUD. To enter, you need a character and a password that identifies your alter ego. Let's create the new you.

Creating Your Alter Ego

Since you don't have a character yet, it's time to make up a name for your alter ego. Don't feel pressured here—if you pick a stupid name, you can always delete the character later and, since we're only doing this for demonstration purposes, it doesn't really matter. We'll cover picking a name in Chapter 4.

To create your alter ego, type in the name of your character at the

By what name do you wish to be known?

line. Try not to use your own name, or the name of a famous superhero, or the name of some deity, or even a common name. Try something unique. Here, we've chosen the name Dorle, which is backwards for Elrod, my usual MUD character's name. Type your name and press Enter (or Return). You should see something like this:

By what name do you wish to be known? Dorle
Did I get that right, Dorle (Y/N)? y

Some MUDs require you to register a new character through e-mail. If you come to a MUD that does this, follow the instructions. Soon, you will get a name and password through your e-mail account.

If you've picked a name that no one else has used, you should see something similar to above. However, if you've picked a name that someone else is already using, you'll see this:

By what name do you wish to be known? Dorle
Password:

Why is everything so darn slow? Sometimes when you log onto a MUD, especially if you connect at night, the MUD may appear to be in slow motion. Everything you type seems to take forever to show up, and when you hit the Enter (or Return) key, there's a noticeable amount of time before the MUD responds. What's going on? Well, you've just experienced the wonderful phenomenon called *lag*. Since MUDs allow multiple users, they must split their computing resources between everyone. If lots of people are logged on at one time, the MUD can become overloaded, slowing down to a crawl.

How do you avoid lag? The best way is to limit your MUDding to off-peak times such as early morning or late aftenoon. Sure, you may not run into as many people, but you'll probably have more fun because you aren't spending half your time waiting for the MUD to respond.

Here, the MUD has recognized the name "Dorle" and is asking you to confirm your identity with Dorle's password. Whoops! Press Enter (or Return) and you'll be disconnected from the MUD. Telnet in again and start over.

If you've picked a unique name and you've spelled it right, press "y" to confirm that you want that name. You'll then be prompted for a password:

Give me a password for Dorle:
Please retype password:

HOT TIP

Caution: Pick a unique password that is not the same as the password you use to log into your regular computer account. I'm not kidding! Even though most MUD wizards are pretty scrupulous, some aren't and may check their password files and try to log onto your real computer account. This could cost you big bucks if you are paying for your account, or it could get you in trouble.

Once you've selected a password (and made sure to have some way of remembering it), retype your password to confirm it. You'll then be asked a series of questions about your character:

What is your sex (M/F)? m

This question is not asking your real-life sex, but what sex you want your character to be. One of the really cool things about these virtual worlds is that you can really be whatever the heck you want to be! There's no reason why you have to be a man on a MUD just because you are one in real life. Also, some MUDs go even farther and allow you to choose "neuter" or "other" for your gender. Be creative!

After choosing your sex, you should see this:

Select a class:
[C]leric
[T]hief
[W]arrior
Class: w

This question has nothing to do with your income or grade in school. Most MUDs group player characters into different classes with different abilities, strengths and weaknesses. The three basic classes of MUD player characters are: Cleric, Thief and Warrior. The Cleric possesses healing strengths but may not be able to use certain types of magic or weapons. The Thief is a dastardly rouge type who is often fast and stealthy but is not particularly strong. The Warrior, your basic Arnold Schwarzennegger character type, is strong, deadly and not too bright. Some MUDs may add classes, depending on the setting, with Paladins, Mages and many other types of characters. Choose carefully, because it may determine how you will fare later in the game.

```
                    Welcome to Games of Death

                         G.O.D. MUD 1.0


        Welcome all and one to the Games of Death MUD where death lurks
behind every corner and you face unsurmountable odds to survive!  If you are
a coward or are afraid of a hardy challenge then do not login for this
game is not a place for the weak of heart.  Only the strong and brave wander
through these realms.  Monsters of all shapes and sizes will attempt to
relieve you of your only precious possesion, your life.  But do NOT fear
for your sword is your best friend and sorcery is your tool.

------------------------------------------------------------------------------
   This is one MUD where the player file will NEVER be deleted.
------------------------------------------------------------------------------
```

Figure 3-3: *Games of Death welcomes you.*

That's it! Once you've selected your character type, you're almost in the game. The welcome screen greets you in Figure 3-3.

Once you've read the screen (and decided not to run away!) press Enter (or Return) and the main MUD menu appears (see Figure 3-4).

```
Welcome to Games of Death MUD!
0) Exit from G.O.D. MUD.
1) Enter the game.
2) Enter description.
3) Read the background story.
4) Change password.
5) Delete this character.
```

Figure 3-4: *Choices at the Games of Death menu.*

Option 1 allows your newly created character to enter the game. Don't use it yet—it's probably a good idea to look at the other options first. Option 2 allows you to describe your new self. Again, this doesn't have to have anything to do with what your real-life self looks like. Instead, this description is what others on the MUD see when they look at your character. You can change this later if you don't like it, but let's try giving ol' Dorle a description.

```
Enter the text you'd like others to see when they look at you.
Terminate with a '@'.

]A tall, muscular man with a perfect tan, rippling muscles, and the bluest

]eyes you have ever seen. To see Dorle is to fall in love instantly and to

]hear his laugh is to hear the angels sing.

]@
```

Figure 3-5: *Dorle's description.*

Figure 3-5 shows what I entered.

Actually, I cheated here—this is what I look like. *Not!* Anyway, you type your description at the] and press Enter (or Return) when you reach the edge of the screen (there's no word wrap like in a word processor). Type a 2–3 line description and a @ on a blank line to indicate that you're done. If you typed everything in OK, you'll go back to the menu again.

Option 3 allows you to read the MUD's background—who developed it, who put it up and sometimes even a little information on the theme. Option 4 allows you to change your password, and Option 5 allows you to delete your character if you're sick of playing that persona. Option 0 disconnects you from the MUD and puts you back in your host computer.

```
Welcome to the land of G.O.D. MUD!  May your visit here be...
Interesting.

Welcome.  This is your new G.O.D. MUD character.  You can now earn
gold,
experience, and lots more...
Sun Valley City - The Future
You enter through a warp in time and now stand in the city over two thousand
years in the future.  You can not believe the sight that befalls your eyes.
The gaming facilities are in ruins!  Sections of road and pavement are torn
up as if by a tremendous force.  You make a frantic run for the portal, but you
are too late.  The portal has closed up and with it your hopes of returning to
your family and friends.
This object is BAD!  If you see it, there must be a bug in the game.  Please
report it immediately using the BUG command.
An automatic teller machine has been installed in the wall here.
--- Bulletin Boards are located UP from here ---
A large fountain carved from blue-streaked marble is here, bubbling merrily.

>
```

Figure 3-6: *Entering Games of Death.*

OK, now that you've made a description of yourself and have done the prudent thing by checking out what the other menu options do, let's get on with it! Press 1 to enter Games of Death and hold on to your virtual hats!

Entering the MUD

After pressing 1 to enter the game, you should see something like Figure 3-6.

This is what you'll see when you first enter the MUD. Let's break it down. First, after the greeting, the top line is the "name" of the "room" that you've entered. Next comes the description—what the room looks like, sounds like, feels like and smells like to you, the character. Always try to read this part carefully; clues are often hidden in the middle of a long description and are easily glanced over if you're hurrying to get on with the game.

Following the description you'll see a listing of the contents of the room. These contents could include people, monsters, other characters, treasure, trash—whatever is in the room that you could potentially interact with. Animate objects, be they other characters, monsters or other MUD creatures (often referred to as *mobs*, short for mobiles) are usually followed with a word or two about their state—sleeping, sitting, searching, etc. Objects, however, often are just referred to by their name: short sword, wand of invisibility, blue mushroom, etc. For example, upon entering the Games of Death MUD we see a large, blue-streaked marble fountain bubbling merrily away. Finally, at the end of everything is the ">" character—the prompt where you type all your interactions with the MUD.

What to do? The best place to start on any new MUD is the help system. Not surprisingly, the command for help is "help." Type **help** at the prompt and press Enter (or Return). Figure 3-7 shows the help screen.

```
> help
---------------------------------------------------------------------------------
Movement:                            | Communication:
NORTH SOUTH EAST WEST UP DOWN        | SAY GSAY SHOUT HOLLER TELL ASK WHISPER
LOOK EXITS ENTER LEAVE               | MAIL RECEIVE CHECK GOSSIP GRATS AUCTION
SLEEP WAKE REST SIT STAND            | NOTELL NOSHOUT NOGOSSIP NOGRATS NOAUCTION
(LOCK UNLOCK OPEN CLOSE)             |
---------------------------------------------------------------------------------
Objects:                             | Information:
GET DROP JUNK DONATE PUT GIVE WEAR   | SCORE HELP INFO WHO NEWS TIME WEATHER
GRAB INVENTORY EQUIPMENT REMOVE      | WHERE CONSIDER LEVELS WIZLIST IMMLIST
EXAMINE EAT DRINK TASTE SIP POUR     | CREDITS TOGGLE FLAGS WIZHELP
---------------------------------------------------------------------------------
Combat:                              | Utility:
KILL WIELD FLEE ASSIST TRACK         | ! BUG IDEA TYPO QUIT SAVE BRIEF COMPACT
(KICK BASH RESCUE BACKSTAB CAST)     | TITLE NOSUMMON COMMANDS SOCIALS DISPLAY
---------------------------------------------------------------------------------
Further information available by HELP <keyword>, keyword being a command or
(for example) one of the following:

SOCIAL SHOPS INNS CLERIC WARRIOR THIEF MAGIC SPELLS LINK
```

Figure 3-7: *Games of Death help screen.*

HOT TIP

The area where you enter the MUD is almost always a safe haven where you can loiter, reading news and help files for as long as you want without fearing death. So, stick around and try to find out as much as you can before heading blindly into the fray—you have nothing to lose.

Read this carefully—it provides some useful information on how you as a player interact with the MUD. In fact, knowing the right command can sometimes mean the virtual life or death of your character. On a MUD, knowledge almost always equals power.

The help screen is a list of all the commands that are available to you on the MUD, organized into topical sections. For example, if you wanted some help on communicating with other players, you'd look in the "Communication" block and notice that there are 18 different commands you can use to communicate with other players. You probably might want to say something to someone at one point or another, so let's check out how the say command works. Figure 3-8 shows what we see when we ask for help on the say command.

```
> help say
SAY TELL ASK WHISPER SHOUT YELL HOLLER '
If you consider communicating with other beings, you might be understood
better if you start your sentences with either say, tell, whisper or shout.

<say | shout | holler> <string>
<tell | whisper | ask> <player> <string>

> say Hey, does anyone know how to get to Oz?
> tell uncle hi, how are you?

You can use ' as a shorthand for say, as in: ' hello there.

Shout broadcasts your message to everyone is your geographic zone.  Holler
broadcasts to everyone in the game but costs 20 movement points.  You must
be level 2 before you can use shout and yell.

See also: GOSSIP AUCTION GSAY NOREPEAT QSAY

>
```

Figure 3-8: *Help on the say command.*

Whew! That's a lot of information about a simple command. Let's start from the top. The words in bold represent commands related to say. Next, the help system often gives some advice about using the command. Here a slightly sarcastic remark tells you the advantages of using say, rather than shout or holler to communicate. Next, the syntax lines show you how to use the command. The part in brackets "<>" tells you that say, shout and holler are similar commands and the following part in brackets <string> stands for the words you want to speak.

Following the syntax line is an example or two about how to use the command. After that, you learn that "'" can stand in for say and that you can't use some of the more powerful commands until you've reached a higher level. Finally, the help system recommends some related commands that may be of interest.

Now, you may want to check out some of the other items in the help system, such as the movement and objects commands, so that you're ready when we start walking around.

Next, let's check out one of the most important commands on the MUD—the news command. By typing **news** you can get the most up-to-date information on the MUD—what's going on with the wizards, what to do and not to do, things that may change and things you need to be kept up to date on. See Figure 3-9 for a glimpse at the Games of Death news.

```
> news
                         THE CIRCLEMUD HERALD
              "We addict players for their own enjoyment."
                          September 19, 1993


NEW COMMANDS AND NEW MUD BEHAVIOR:
---------------------------------

**  Your character no longer gains move points with age.  However, age
    does still affect your HMV gains.  Also, move point modifier objects
    now work correctly.

**  You can now use "all" and "all.x" very generally with the get, put,
    drop, junk, donate, give, wear and remove commands.  Type HELP GET
    for more info.

**  The "track" function will show you the first step on the shortest
    path to anyone in the game.

**  If you drop your link for more than 1 hour, you will be force-rented
    at 25% greater than normal rent prices.  If you don't have enough
    money to rent with, your most valuable items will be junked until

*** Press return to continue, q to quit ***
```

Figure 3-9: *The Circlemud Herald brings you Games of Death news.*

As you can see, there's a lot of important stuff here. Make it a habit to check the news periodically whenever you're playing a MUD.

Getting the Lay of the Land

By now, you're probably more than ready to start your adventure. Let's go!

Mapping Your World

Mapping a MUD is one of the most important skills you can learn. A map tells you where you are, where you've been and often helps you discover nifty stuff like secret passages and paths you might have missed.

How do you make a map?

1. Get a piece of graphing paper. If you don't have graph paper, any lined paper will do.
2. Draw a square to represent where you are. Also, it might help to draw a compass in the corner to remind you what direction is north.
3. Use the exits command to find the exits from the room you're in. Draw lines from your beginning square representing the different directions that the exits go.

4. Go though one of the exits and draw another square representing your new location. Check the exits, draw your exit lines and move along, repeating this procedure as you go. Simple, eh?

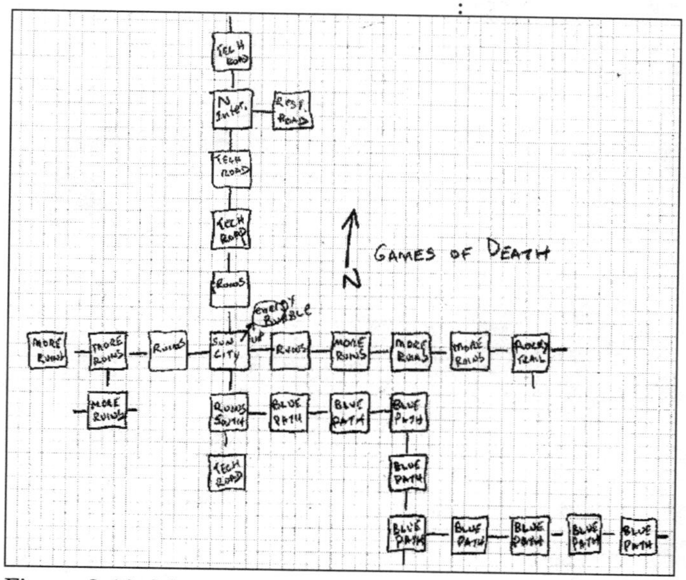

Figure 3-10: *My attempt at mapping the beginnings of Games of Death.*

You may want to remember a few tips while you're drawing your map. First, make sure to leave enough space so that if you discover a room and need to add it later, you can. Next, take care that your lines are long enough between your "rooms" to allow for any twisty passages you might encounter. Finally, if you come up with a better system, use it! A map is there to help you figure out where you are, and if you use a different method, that's fine.

Let's take a walk out of the main room, through some ruins, and take a magical, glowing blue path to a portal between worlds where we'll jump into the main town of Midgaard. Sounds cool, huh?

Let's head south first. Type **s** or **south** and press Enter (or Return). Figure 3-11 illustrates what you might see.

```
>s

Ruins - South

You are surrounded by the the ruins of the once proud city. The devestation seems
to be spread out in a north-south direction. You suspect that a tornado hit
the city many years ago. You wonder why the city's weather control systems did
not respond in time to prevent the disaster. A glowing blue path catches you
eye in the east, but a huge floating tower to the south is even more amazing.
The corpse of a tiny maintenence robot is lying here.
Chuck the sentry is here, fighting a dust cloud.
A dust cloud is here, fighting Chuck.
>
```

Figure 3-11: *Heading through the ruins.*

Wow! We walked right into a fight! Chances are, nobody will be fighting when you take this tour, but I'm including this directly from a log of one of my visits to Games of Death so that you can get a feeling what MUDding is really like.

Generally, it's not a good idea to interfere with another player when they're fighting unless they ask for help, so let's press on. First we'll check to see what exits are available from this room by using the exits command:

> exits

Obvious exits:
North - Sun Valley City - The Future
East - Glowing Blue Path
South - Tech Road 1 - South

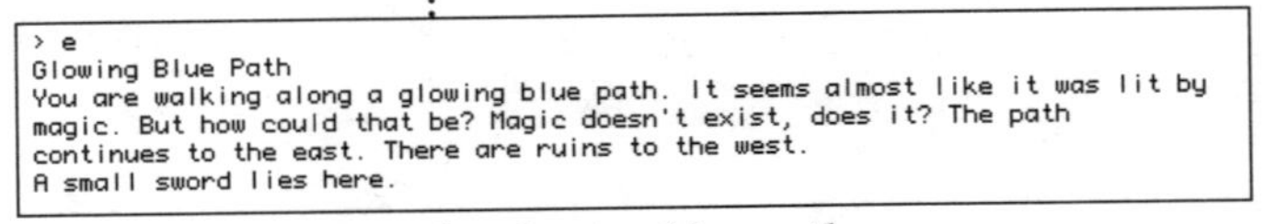

Figure 3-12: *Down the glowing blue path.*

You'll see that north is where we just came from, going east takes us to the Glowing Blue Path, and going south takes us to Tech Road 1. Let's go east.

You'll notice that "A small sword lies here." Great! We could use that later to fend off any monsters that may come our way. Let's pick it up. You can do so by typing the get command.

> get sword
You get a small sword.

Now you have the sword. However, "getting" it just picks it up. If you want to have it ready to use when you need it, you need to "wield" it. Type **wield sword** to ready it for fighting.

> wield sword
You wield a small sword.

We're ready to roll. In the interests of saving time, we're going to boogie into town and not linger on the path. If you want, you can come back later and look around, but for now let's get to where the action is. The directions to the Portal Between Worlds are as follows: **e e s s e e e e e e**.

I'm sure that line probably doesn't make a lick of sense to you at this point. In fact, it's MUD shorthand for directions, meaning that you should go east two times, go south twice and then go east again six more times. Often, when you ask someone for directions on a MUD, this is how they'll give them to you.

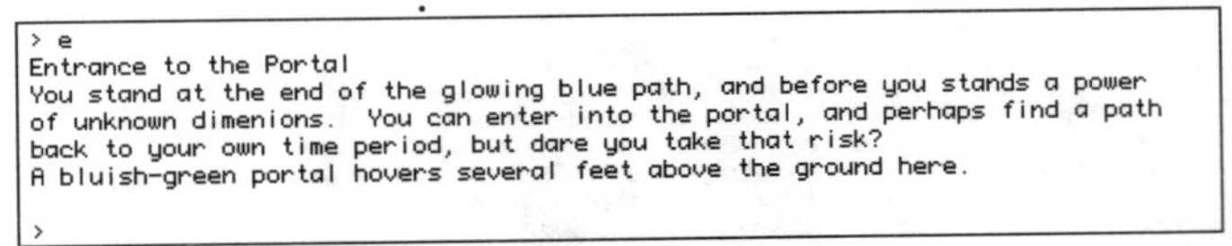

Figure 3-13: *At the entrance to the portal.*

If all went well, and you followed the directions above, you should be at the glowing portal. See Figure 3-13.

Going east takes you into the portal. See Figure 3-14.

```
> e
In Between Realities
You enter into the portal!  You are standing in a reality between realities.
Strange ghostly forms appear in the air before you.  Are they phantoms or
travellers in this strange dimension?  You get the feeling that paths lie to
many different worlds from here.

>
```

Figure 3-14: *In-between realities.*

Finally, it's time to travel into the new world. Go north to enter the town of Midgaard. You should see something like Figure 3-15.

```
> n
Market Square
   You are standing on the market square, the famous Square of Midgaard.
A large, peculiar looking statue is standing in the middle of the square.
Roads lead in every direction, north to the temple square, south to the
common square, east and westbound is the main street.
A rather dubious looking piece of meat is on the ground here.
A Peacekeeper is standing here, ready to jump in at the first sign of trouble.
A Peacekeeper is standing here, ready to jump in at the first sign of trouble.

>
```

Figure 3-15: *The Market Square of Midgaard.*

You've arrived! From here, you can explore the town in relative comfort, checking out the shops and various guilds around town. Midgaard is filled with strange people, twisty paths and dangerous dark corners, so make sure to keep a map of your travels as you go.

Here's where I let go of your hand and send you off to an untimely death...er...I mean, fabulous adventure! Your first task will be to get a hold of some money somehow—at this point, you're a penniless character with a wimpy sword. Once you get some cash, you can outfit yourself at the different stores in Midgaard—there's a bakery for food, an armorer for armor and clothing, and a weapons shop to buy your implements of destruction.

How do you get money? You'll have to find that out for yourself. You might start by walking around and talking to people. Use the say command to communicate. Usually, a simple "Hi, I'm a cashless newbie, can you help me out?" can get you some spare change. If not, finding objects and selling them back to the appropriate stores can net you some money. The only way you'll ever learn is to get out there and find out for yourself. Remember, you can always type **help** in case you need to know a command to use, and asking other players can sometimes point you in the right direction. If you're really lucky, you may be able to get a player to take you under his or her wing and get a guided tour of the MUD. On the other hand, you may stumble around blindly and be slaughtered by a local monster. Who can know for sure? That's the beauty of virtual worlds—the interactive element, knowing that you're online with people from all over the world lends a quality to the game that you just can't find with computer opponents. Have fun, and when you're ready to exit, just type **quit** to go back to the real world. Once you're back, journey to the next chapter to find out the nitty-gritty on MUD history, terminology and general life lessons in getting around and making a success of yourself.

Tracking the Wild MUD

If your adventure on Games of Death has whet your appetite for more MUDding, but you don't know where to go to find more MUDs, look no further! Several dedicated people have been compiling directories of all the MUDs on the Internet. Here's how to get them:

World Wide Web

Amberyl's MUD Resource Collection

http://www.cis.upenn.edu/~lwl/mudinfo.html

Links to just about every MUD resource available on the Internet, all painstakingly organized and indexed by Lydia Lebig, who's also known as Amberyl on various MUDs. MUD lists, ftp sites, WWW MUD archives and just about anything else you could want you can find here.

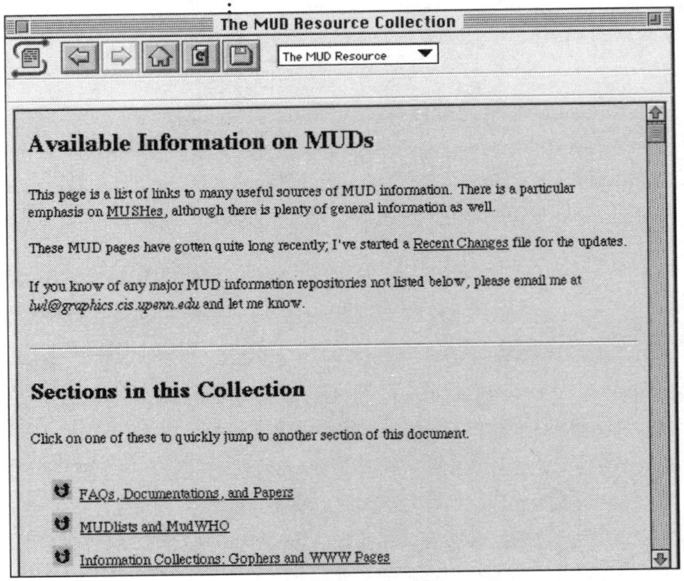

Figure 3-16: *Amberyl's MUD Resource Collection home page.*

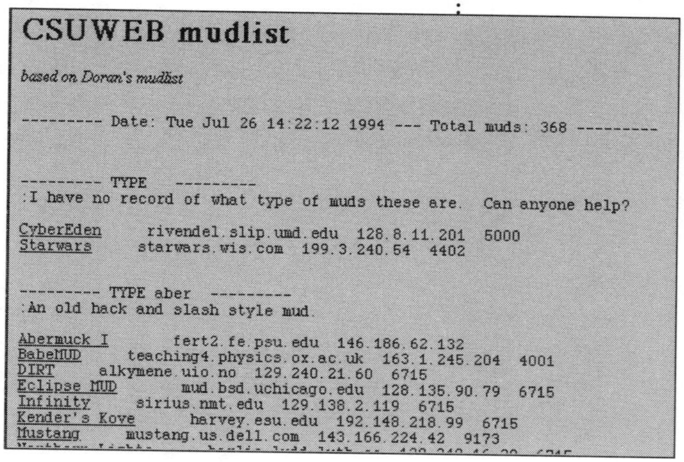

Figure 3-17: *A nicely hyperlinked MUD list.*

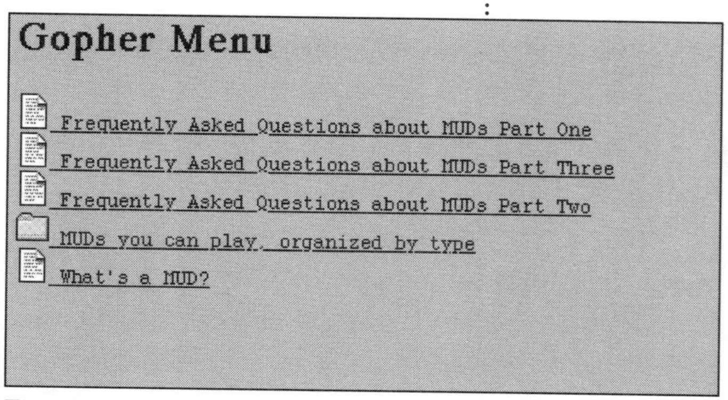

Figure 3-18: *The teal.csn.org gopher directory.*

Doran's MUD List—WWW version

http://csugrad.cs.vt.edu/soc/dorans.html

You can access just about any MUD in the world from this collection of over 500 different MUDs. This site is based on Doran's MUD List, considered by many to be the definitive MUD resource.

E-Mail

Doran's MUD List

e-mail address: awozniak@geordi.calpoly.edu

This gran'pappy of all MUD lists is a list of all the MUDs on the Internet, organized by type. It's published about every month or so and you can be pretty sure that if a MUD isn't on this list, either it doesn't exist or it doesn't want to be found. Get your own copy by sending a message with the word ISSUE in the Subject: field to awozniak@geordi.calpoly.edu.

Gopher

MUD: Multi User Dimension

gopher server: teal.csn.org
path: /Databases/Games and Fun/MUD: Multi-User Dimension

This Gopher server contains the MUD-FAQ, the definitive online document that answers all your MUDding questions. You'll also find a handy list of MUDs, organized by theme, that you can jump to directly from Gopher.

Virtual Spaces: MUD
gopher server: actlab.rtf.utexas.edu
path: Virtual Environments (MUD, MOO, MUSH, etc.)
The Actlab Gopher server is considered by many to be the ultimate repository of MUD information. MUD lists, texts on MUDding and connections to MUDs abound in this voluminous site.

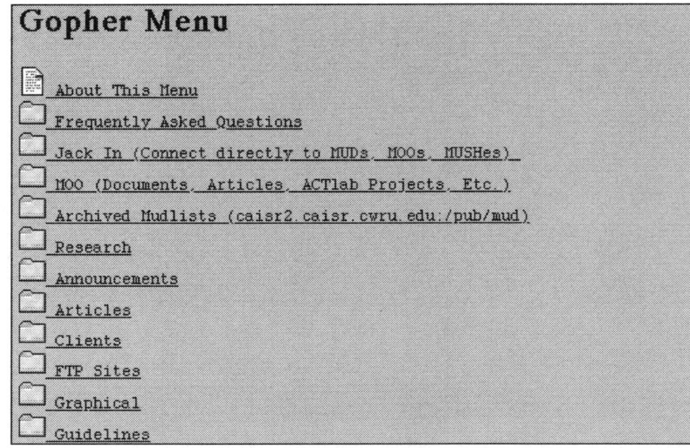

Figure 3-19: *MUD info galore at the ActLab Gopher.*

Moving On

That wasn't so bad, was it? Now that you've gotten a taste of what MUDding is like, it's time to roll up our sleeves and dig into some of the bigger issues. You may think I left you hanging at the end of this chapter—I did. Think of it as a virtual kick in the pants to get out there and experience the joys (and terrors) of discovery.

In the next chapter, we'll examine how to make your game playing more enjoyable and your online life a bit easier. We'll look at the differences between the two major MUD types (DikuMUD and LPMud) and how these differences affect the way you play the game. We'll look at how to build up a character though careful name selection and description. Finally, we'll examine living (and dying) in a virtual world.

So get ready—I'm not though with you yet!

4

MUDS: MULTIPLAYER ADVENTURES

Now that you've gotten your virtual feet wet in a real MUD (and hopefully lived to tell about it!), it's time to take a more in-depth look at different types of MUDs. As you'll remember from Chapter 1, all MUDs are not created the same. You've got your DikuMUDs and your LPMuds, your MUSHes, MUCKs and MOOs, and a host of other types. They're all Net-connected "places" where many people can meet online and interact. However, that's where the similarity ends. With literally hundreds of different virtual communities on the Net, making generalizations about them is nearly impossible. We can make some sense of it if we divide virtual worlds into two groups: MUDs and virtual communities. Generally, MUDs are games and virtual communities emphasize personal interaction between players. With that distinction in mind, let's go MUDding.

We'll begin our journey into the more esoteric aspects of MUDding by tracing the history of the oldest and most popular types of MUDs: DikuMUDs and LPMuds. If you've followed along up to this point, you already know a little bit about DikuMUDs from our jaunt around Games of Death. Let's take a closer look.

DikuMUD: The Compromise

DikuMUDs are quickly becoming one of the most popular types of MUDs. Currently, there are over 60 DikuMUDs in operation, second only to the over 100 LPMuds on the Internet. DikuMUDs are popular because they combine social interaction with fighting, a delicate balance that they pull off pretty well.

MUDs' Medieval Roots You've probably noticed by now that most of this book's MUD examples seem to come from medieval- or fantasy-type MUDs. While there are MUDs based on just about any type of world you can imagine, the first ones were based on fantasy role-playing games, and these roots run deep throughout the MUD worlds. Just remember that no matter what type of world you find yourself in, the basics are the same. What you learn in this chapter will apply to just about any MUD.

DikuMUDs were developed around 1990 at the Department of Computer Science at the University of Copenhagen. In Danish, that's Datalogisk Institut ved Kbenhavns Universitet, or DIKU. Until then, AberMUDs (one of the earliest MUD forms) had been the norm. But these were limited because of their small size and lack of easy expandability. AberMUDs accommodated about 18 players at a time, which wasn't a problem in the early days of the Net, but became a big issue as more and more people came online. Besides these technical limitations, AberMUDs were set up so that most game play was limited to cruising around, mapping the game and killing monsters. There weren't many commands for interacting with other players besides the plain-vanilla say and shout commands. AberMUDs were designed so that one person playing alone could walk around and kick butt without ever having to really interact with the other players.

DikuMUDs were designed as a compromise between the purely social, chat-type MUDs and the lone warrior, hack-and-slash AberMUDs. They retained most of the gaming aspects of AberMUDs while adding features that encouraged people to interact and work together, arriving at a pretty successful middle ground. On the technical end, DikuMUDs are designed to be faster and more efficient programs, making them more fun to play. The new design proved so successful that DikuMUD development still continues, with a DikuMUD II version in the works as well as the variants CircleMUD, MercMud and SillyMUD. If you want to know more about DikuMUDs, visit the Darkside DikuMUD home page at **http://gothic.acs.csulb.edu:8080/Diku/index.html**

Figure 4-1: *The Darkside DikuMUD home page.*

LPMuds: Programmable MUDs

Another branch off the AberMUD tree is the LPMud. LPMuds offer a programming language called LPC to allow players to add their own areas, monsters and features to the MUD. While this feature is usually reserved for the more advanced players, it has allowed LPMuds to go places where MUDs had never gone before. Gone are the older static worlds where everything stayed the same. Now, MUDs can more or less expand forever, with new areas being added as players rise in skill and learn how to code in LPC.

Where did LPMuds come from? Their name gives a hint: The LP stands for Lars Pensjö, creator of the first LPMud, Genesis. Most of Genesis was taken from the original AberMUD code, which was freely available on the Net. With the addition of an online programming language, LPMud took off. As Lars continued working on a newer version of LPMud, others grew impatient and hacked the original

LPMud code to produce their own versions, including CD, LPC4, MudOS and LP-German. Not all of these survived to the present day, but you'll still see different flavors of LPMud lumped together in MUD lists. For more information on LPMuds, visit the Lysator WWW home page located at **http://www.lysator.liu.se:7500/nobw/mud/main.html**

For a beginning MUDder, most of the distinctions between LPMuds and DikuMUDs don't make much difference when it comes to playing the game. Since DIKU and LPMuds share a common ancestor in AberMUD, the basic commands are the same. You need to learn how to create an interesting character, how to interact with others on the MUD, how to get the lay of the land and how to fight the monsters that come your way. That's what we're here to do. Let's get started.

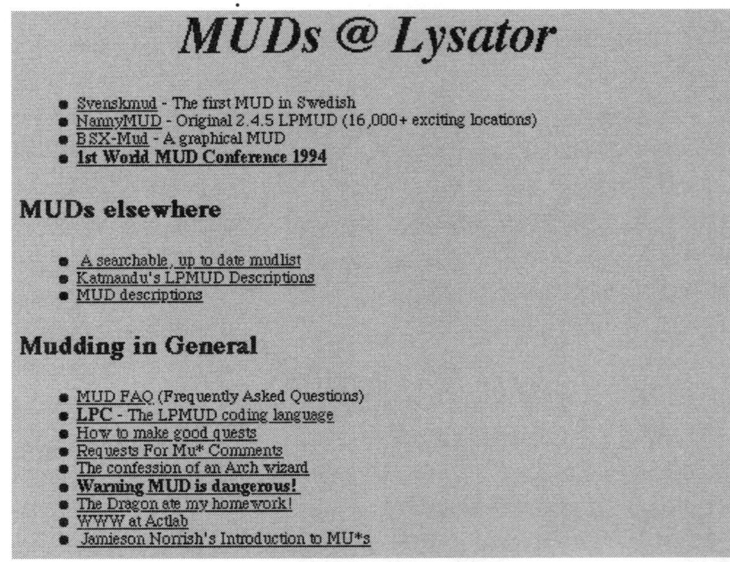

Figure 4-2: *The Lysator WWW home page.*

Making a Name for Yourself

You really can't do much about your name or appearance in real life (unless you're Cher, but that's a whole different book). But in the text-based virtual reality of MUDs, you can be whomever you want to be. So what if you're a six-foot-four weight lifter in real life? On a MUD you could be a diminutive good witch, a powerful warrior or a scrawny, sneaky thief. Nothing screams "newbie" more than a character without a description or, worse yet, a boring, generic description. On a MUD, first impressions can mean the difference between finding an ally for a quest or getting whacked over the head with a mace.

Picking a Good Name

Picking a good name is the cornerstone of a good character. First of all, do not, I repeat, DO NOT pick a name like Mercenary, King, IceMonster or Snake—these names probably will occur as monsters on the MUD and could lead to some pretty ugly misunderstandings. Just think—what would you do if you saw something like "Snake sizes you up" while you were playing? You'd probably not take the time to talk to the Snake—you'd either run away or whack it over the head as fast as you could. These might be good common-sense responses, but if Snake happens to be a newbie with a bad name, you could cause some hard feelings later on.

Help! That Command Doesn't Work! Perhaps the most fascinating aspect of MUDding is the variety of worlds you can explore. There are probably thousands of different MUDs on the Internet, each with its own unique settings and characters. Unfortunately, even though all this variety can keep things pretty interesting, it also makes it impossible to cover every possible type of MUD system in a short book. I've had to compromise a bit. While most of the commands you'll learn in this chapter apply to nearly every MUD system, you'll probably encounter MUDs in which things don't work exactly as you see them here. That's fine. Just about every MUD in existence has a help command that tells you what commands to use and how. Use it!

Likewise, don't pick a name from a book, TV show or movie. People may expect you to be able to do things you aren't prepared to do.

So what kind of name should you pick? Be creative and tailor your MUD name to the overall theme of the MUD. If you're on a more traditional medieval-themed MUD, try something heroic if you're a warrior, or something mysterious if you're a mage. If you're on a MUD with a science-fiction theme, try thinking about a name that sounds other-worldly. To get an idea what kind of name might be suitable, log on as a guest and look at what kinds of names other characters have. You'll get the hang of it pretty quickly if you pay attention.

Descriptions: Your Virtual Body

Describing yourself is the next challenge. Depending on the MUD, you may or may not be able to enter a description of yourself. Some MUDs use canned descriptions for characters that reflect their skill levels:

Ankar the Newbie, Debron the Ur-Mage and so on. However, if the MUD allows you to enter a description of yourself, it's time to get creative.

Your description is what people see when they type **look at <your name>** when you walk into the room. On DikuMUDs, the main menu gives you the option of changing your description every time you log onto the MUD. On AberMUDs, you can type **C DESC** while you're in the game to make a description for yourself. On most LPMuds, you can use the describe command to create or change your description. If these commands don't work, just ask another player how to describe yourself by saying something like "Hi! How do I describe myself?" You can also use the help or info command to find more.

Like choosing a name, writing a good description takes both creativity and common sense. Try to match your description with your character type. Warriors will probably not be "short, thin humans with stick-like legs and a concave chest," and Mages probably won't look like bodybuilders. Try to include some details in your description that appeal to senses other than sight. A note about an "odor of wood smoke" for a character who comes from a small village can go far to evoke a "mood." Since a description is supposed to reflect what other characters experience when looking at you, try to avoid musings on your past or current thought processes. This kind of information should come from interaction—there's no way that someone looking at you is going to know that you "often are quick in a fight and eager to kill everyone who walks in your path." Some of the best characters are created off-line—write a description *before* you go MUDding.

After you've described yourself and have connected to a MUD, examine yourself to see if your description works. If it does, then it's time to move on. If not, go back and change it.

Gathering the Goods

Now you're ready to outfit yourself. Depending on the MUD, this may be an easy proposition or a major quest, but without weapons, armor and something to light your way through those cold, dark places, you won't get far.

Some MUDs provide you with a "newbie kit" when you first log on and create a character. These kits contain everything that the newbie adventurer needs to survive, usually including a low-powered weapon, rudimentary armor and maybe a torch or a lantern. With these, you can survive long enough to gain some experience and gold and then purchase some decent stuff.

Other MUDs have "donation rooms" near the entrance to the MUD containing other players' cast-off gear. Their loss is your gain if you find one of these rooms, which usually contain better-than-average stuff. On the other hand, you may not find anything at all.

Most likely, you're going to have to beg, borrow or steal some gold or equipment to outfit yourself. You'd better sharpen those interpersonal skills if this is your only option.

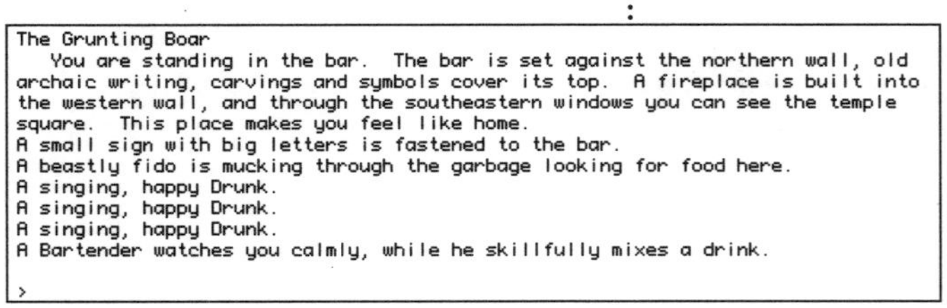

Figure 4-3: *Hanging out at the Grunting Boar Inn.*

Usually, it works like this: you've arrived on a new MUD and you've got no armor, no weapon and no gold to buy them with. Take a look around the room to see if anyone else is there; to do this, type **look**. If there's no one around, look for an exit (by typing **exits**) and head off in a promising direction. Look for towns or inns—that's where people tend to congregate.

Hopefully, after a little while, you'll find a friendly looking fellow adventurer. Introduce yourself and try a little humility. "Hi!" you might say, "I'm new here and was wondering if you might be able to spare some coins?" Usually, an appeal like this works. Everyone else on the MUD is there to have fun, and most remember what it's like to be the new babe in the virtual woods. Even those who have nothing to spare often can point you in the right direction.

Let's say you're in town and someone has given you some cash. Your next step is to find one of the many shops that sell equipment. Towns vary, but usually there's an armorer, a weapons shop and a general store that sells torches, food and other sundries. Look around, making sure to keep a map so you can find your way back. Once you've found a store, try typing **list** to get a list of the available goods. If that doesn't work, there's usually a sign on the wall with instructions on using the store (try typing **read sign**).

```
The Armory
   The armory with all kinds of armors on the walls and in the window.  You
see helmets, shields and chain mails.  To the north is the main street.
On the wall is a small note.
A beastly fido is mucking through the garbage looking for food here.
An Armorer stands here displaying his shiny new (and previously owned) armors.

> list
You can buy:
A pair of leather pants for 150 gold coins.
A leather cap for 150 gold coins.
A studded leather jacket for 500 gold coins.
A shield for 100 gold coins.
A breast plate for 18000 gold coins.

>
```

Figure 4-4: *Some of the goods available at the Midgaard Armory.*

Choose your goods carefully. It's best to make sure that you have at least one piece of armor, one weapon and one torch or lantern. Don't blow all your cash on one super item and leave yourself vulnerable.

Once you've gotten your stuff, it's time to put it all on. First, type **inventory.** You should get a list of everything you're carrying and a message like the one in Figure 4-5.

As you can see, our intrepid adventurer has managed to procure a weapon (small sword), some armor (chain mail, leather cap and boots) and a light source (brass lantern). That's a good start.

Armor must be worn to be effective. Type **wear all** to put on all your gear. Type **wield small sword** or **wield sword** to prepare your character to fight. That's it! Now you're ready to start your adventure!

```
Main Street
   You are on the main street passing through the City of Midgaard.  South of
here is the entrance to the Armory, and the bakery is to the north.  East of
here is the market square.
An oozing green gelatinous blob is here, sucking in bits of debris.

> inventory

Elrod is carrying the following:

a small sword
a brass lantern
chain mail
leather cap
leather boots

>
```

Figure 4-5: *Inventory list.*

Common Commands for Newbies

Table 4-1 lists some of the most common MUD commands. Commands differ somewhat from MUD to MUD, so use the help command if you find that one of these doesn't work.

Command	Description
examine <thing>	Looks at something more closely. May or may not reveal more than simply looking.
equipment	Some MUDs use this command to tell you what armor you're wearing. Some accomplish the same thing using the inventory command.
get <thing>	Takes an object and puts it in your inventory.
help	The most important command of all. Describes commands and gives background on the MUD.
info	Some MUDs use this command for supplementary information. This is not a universal command.
inventory	Lists your stuff.
look	Describes the physical appearance of the room you're in. Look will also often tell you what other players, monsters and objects are there with you.
look at <thing>	Describes <thing>. Useful for examining objects or other players.
news	Gives current news about the MUD.
north, south, east, west, up, down	Directional commands for moving around the MUD.

say "something"	Says whatever's in quotes so that others in the room can read it. This is what you use to talk to others.
score	Tells you your current state of being.
sit/stand	Lets you sit down and get back up again.
sleep	Allows you to rest if you are hurt.
wear <thing>	Puts an item in your inventory on your body for protection. You usually cannot wear two things in the same place: two pairs of gloves, two hats, etc.
wield <weapon>	Prepares a weapon in your inventory for use.

Table 4-1: *Some common MUD commands.*

Winning Friends & Influencing People

Now that you're ready to go, let's look at some of the basic do's and don'ts of MUD communication. How you conduct yourself is just as important as how many monsters you kill or points you accumulate. The most important thing to remember is that MUDs are multiuser games. Behind every character there's a real-life person on the other end of the line. Learning to communicate effectively and to behave in the context of the whole MUD community won't just make your virtual life easier—it'll make everyone else's experience more pleasant as well.

Say It: Speaking & Shouting

There are several ways of speaking to other players. As we've seen so far, say is the most common command, but other commands give you more flexibility. Check help for some common commands. See Figure 4-6.

```
---------------------------------------------
| Communication:
| SAY GSAY SHOUT HOLLER TELL ASK WHISPER
| MAIL RECEIVE CHECK GOSSIP GRATS AUCTION
| NOTELL NOSHOUT NOGOSSIP NOGRATS NOAUCTION
|
---------------------------------------------
```

Figure 4-6: *Common communication commands.*

The tell command allows you to speak to a specific character if there are others in the room. By typing **tell <charactername>** and what you want to say, you can have a person-to-person chat in a crowded bar.

Shout allows you to broadcast to everyone on the MUD. If you shout something, everyone, no matter where, sees your words. Use this command cautiously! Nothing is more annoying than having people shout everything that comes to mind. Shouts of "LEVEL!" or "Where can I find the crystal orb?" can get annoying fast. If others are bothering you with their shouts, use the noshout command to ignore them.

These are the most basic MUD communication commands. Check help to find out if there are more on your MUD. Some MUDs have commands such as gossip and auction that allow you to speak to specific groups of people on the MUD to swap gossip and sell used equipment. Other MUDs have radio-like channels that allow two-way communication between whomever is tuned in to a specific channel. There are many possibilities for communication; try to use as many as you can.

Posing

Emote and pose are commands that let you convey movement and expression to other players in ways that talking just can't. Using these commands, you can smile, frown, hug, kiss, slap, pat, fondle or perform just about any other interpersonal verb you can think of. These commands usually look like this:

> pose smiles at Analar
Dorle smiles at Analar

or

>emote pats Berwin on the head
Dorle pats Berwin on the head

As you can see, the first line shows what I typed at the prompt: the command followed by the action. The second line shows how everyone else in that room sees you performing that action. Some MUDs even have action commands that are like preset emotes, allowing you to do things like this:

>dance with Amberyl
Dorle sweeps Amberyl into his arms and waltzes around the room.

Here, you can see that the dance command is built in, and when I typed it the MUD had me sweep up the lucky Amberyl and waltz around the room. You'll have to look at the MUD's help system to see exactly how to use these commands. Try typing **help pose**, **help emote** or **help actions** for more information.

HOT TIP

Emoting and posing commands are usually *aliased* to ":". This means that you can type a colon (:) and then your action and get the same effect as if you had typed **pose** or **emote**. Say also has an alias, usually a single (') or double quote ("). These aliases promote faster, more natural conversations.

Getting Around

Communicating effectively makes your MUD life more enjoyable, but exploring is where the real challenge begins. If all you want to do is hang around and talk to people, you can always get on the IRC (Internet Relay Chat). What makes MUDs unique is that they are entire virtual worlds waiting to be explored.

The basics of getting around a MUD are simple. Just find an exit and then type the direction to move out of the room you are in and into another room. For example, if you see that there's a door to the south and a room to the west, type **west** to enter the room. That's it, and if you've been following along up until this point, you've probably had plenty of experience moving around. It's easy to be lulled into a false sense of security when you're hanging around in the common areas. Usually these areas are well traveled and safe, free from monsters and evil players who want to kill you. Don't get too settled, though, because you can't advance in rank or gain new skills on a MUD until you've ventured forth and begun to explore the outside worlds.

Some MUDs pretty much let you do your own thing. You can choose to stay in town and explore the sewers as an adventure, or you can head out into the wilderness. There is no ultimate goal in MUDs like these except to advance in rank by gaining more experience points. There might be a few particularly powerful items you can get only by killing lots of monsters and voyaging to far-off corners of the MUD, but these adventures aren't necessary for you to advance in rank.

Other MUDs are built around the concept of quests—predetermined adventures with a beginning and an end you must attain to advance in the game. These quests have more in common with the older, puzzle-solving adventure games because you go into a quest with an idea about what you're supposed to accomplish and advance by solving puzzles and conquering monsters.

Before you head out into the wilderness, develop your skills as much as you can. Some MUDs provide special "newbie areas" or "MUD schools" filled with easy-to-defeat monsters and relatively easy puzzles to solve. If the MUD has one of these, go there right away! You'll gain valuable experience points and treasure while learning the vagaries of the MUD.

Some MUDs also provide special training areas where your character can learn special skills. The training areas vary with character type—mage, thief, warrior—but they let you expend "skill points" to acquire skills that may be special to your class. Take advantage of these areas—usually found in towns—to raise your character's abilities to higher levels.

Whether you are in a MUD that wants you to go on quests, or one that lets you do your own thing, the principles of getting out there and moving around are the same—moving, mapping and careful searching. It's up to you to use these principles to survive.

Fighting: Life & Death

Face it: sooner or later, you have to fight to get anywhere in a MUD. Monsters (also known as "mobs") abound, and usually the way you rise up in level is to gain experience points slaughtering them. Defeating monsters is a task that you'll have to be up to, and it's a task that takes more than just brute force.

Most MUDs use a combat system to determine the outcome of a fight. This means that the MUD takes into account not only your base strength statistics, but also your current hit points, arm or class, and weapon strength to determine whether you can kill a monster.

Term	What It Means
armor class	Your and your opponent's ability to deflect blows. This is usually expressed as a number or ratio. In most cases, the lower the number, the better resistance you have.
corpse	A dead body. Can be examined for loot.

experience	A numeric reward for defeating a monster. Experience points are accumulated to advance to new levels.
hit points	Your ability to withstand damage. The more hit points you have, the more damage you can withstand. Look up your hit points using the score command.
house cleaning	How the MUD deals with dead bodies. Corpses are removed periodically. Some MUDs have special monsters that roam and "eat" corpses and other debris in order to keep the MUD free of grime.
mob	A monster. Pronounced "mobe," it's short for mobile because of MUD monsters' ability to roam.
resistance	A special ability to withstand certain types of attacks. Some mobs may be resistant to magic, others to edged weapons and others to special attacks. The only way to find out is to find out.
special attack	An attack skill that goes beyond the usual methods. Some special attacks are skills taught only by particular character guilds. Others are skills required to counter particular monsters' methods.
weapon strength	The amount of damage that a weapon can do when it hits. Weapon strength usually varies within a range and is modified depending on the armor class of the thing being hit, the dexterity of the character and pure luck. A weapon's strength is often indicated by a number: +1, +3 and so on. The higher the number, the more damage a weapon can do.

Table 4-2: *Fighting jargon.*

If you are familiar with Dungeons and Dragons (or any other fantasy role-playing game that uses statistics and chance to determine the outcome of a battle), you'll feel right at home in a MUD fight. It comes down to this: You start with a basic strength and skill level. Depending on your weapon strength and the monster's armor class, the MUD modifies the chance that your hit will kill the monster. If you happen to be a character who uses magic, the chance that your spell will work depends on your skill level, the spell, and the resistance and strength of the monster.

Sounds pretty complicated, doesn't it? Don't worry. Since MUDs are really just computer programs, the machine takes care of most of the gory details for you. Your skill comes into play in deciding whether to fight, flee or try to pass. If you decide to fight, you must decide what weapon or spell to use. The only way you'll learn what to use is through experience.

Before you start fighting, set your wimpy level (this has nothing to do with Popeye). The wimpy level is the minimum hit points you must have before the computer takes over and sends you fleeing. If you set your wimpy level to 10, you'll automatically flee in a random direction when you have suffered enough damage to reduce your hit points to 10 or fewer. Wimpy can usually save your butt, because it reacts more quickly than you can, helping you run away from a fight so that you can recover. To set your wimpy level, type **wimpy <number of points>** before you get into a fight. The wimpy option is not universal and is not guaranteed to save you, so don't go crying to your local wizard if you get killed.

When you encounter a monster, type **consider <name of monster>**. Most MUDs will then tell you if you have a chance of defeating the monster. If it looks like you can rumble, type **kill <name of monster>** to begin fighting. You should then see a blow-by-blow report of the battle, with each line detailing how much damage your blows and the monster's have done. More often than not, the MUD will not report your damage in numbers, but in phrases like "the monster missed you with his blow" or "the monster hit you HARD with his tail." To check on your progress during the fight, type **score** for a readout of how many hit points you have left. If your hit points are getting dangerously low, type **flee** to run away. You'll flee in a random direction where you can stop and rest. See Figure 4-7 for an example of what happens when you don't use flee!

```
The corridor
   You are standing in a long corridor, decorated with tapestries
depicting old times and old heroes. It leads north and south.
Matt the Royal guard is here on duty.
Jeanette the Royal guard is here on duty.

> kill Matt
You barely pierce Matt the Royal guard.

>
Matt the Royal guard slashes you hard.
That Really did HURT!
You miss Matt the Royal guard with your pierce.

>
Matt the Royal guard slashes you hard.
That Really did HURT!
You miss Matt the Royal guard with your pierce.

> Jeanette the Royal guard roars: 'Protect the Kingdom of Great King Welmar!
BANZAI!!!!!!'
You're stunned, but will probably regain consciousness again.
You are dead!  Sorry...
```

Figure 4-7: *An ignoble ending for Dorle.*

Magic commands vary from MUD to MUD. If you have a magic-using character, use the help command to see how you can use the various spells available. Look for help on commands such as ready, cast and spells to find out more. But since most mages can't survive on magic alone until they reach higher levels, you'll probably pick up more as you explore.

If you're victorious, the monster will die and you'll be awarded a certain number of experience points. However, the booty doesn't end there—most monsters carry some sort of treasure. Once you've killed a monster, type **examine corpse** to list the stuff the monster has. Type **get all from corpse** to loot the body and take what you've won. Then check your score to see how many hit points you have left. If you're low, sleep for a while to regain your points.

Term	What It Means
flee	Run away in a random direction.
hit <name of monster>	Takes one swipe at the monster.
kill <name of monster>	Begins a battle. The computer will take care of most of the details.
score	Reports your current hit point status.
sleep	Lets you rest up after a battle.
wield	Prepares a weapon for battle.
wimpy	Sets the number of experience points that will make your character flee automatically.

Table 4-3: *Fighting commands.*

Depending on the complexity of the MUD, there may be many more commands for fighting than those listed above. In some DikuMUDs you can train for various fighting skills, such as kicking and bashing, and use these skills in battle. Some MUDs require that you use special magic spells. Check the help on your local MUD to find out what special commands you might need to know.

When you've finished a battle, use the score command to check your condition. It will give you information about your hit points that should read something like this:

hitpoints (20/80), mana(50/100)

The ratio in parentheses after "hitpoints" stands for the number of hit points you have left (20) over your maximum hit points (80). On most MUDs, if your total hit points drops below 0, you're dead. Mana is the amount of spell-casting power you have left, also expressed as a ratio over the total amount possible. You lose mana every time you use magic.

On some MUDs you regain hit points just by walking around. In others, you have to rest yourself to regain strength. The fastest way to do this is to go to sleep. Type **sleep** to put your character to bed. Be careful, though—while you're asleep, you're oblivious to what's going on in the outside world. If a monster comes along, you're meat. In fact, all you can really do while you're sleeping is check your score to see how well your rest is coming along. When you have regained all your hit points, type **wake** and then **stand**.

MUD Strategies & Tips

Believe it or not, those are the basics! In a MUD, the computer does the dirty work of handling scores, statistics and outcomes, so you're free to explore new lands, solve puzzles and meet interesting people. The point of this all is to have fun, not to drive yourself nuts. Repeat after me: it's a game. Games are fun. It's a game. Games are. . . . you get the idea.

To make sure the game remains fun, here are some tips on MUDding:

1. You will die. Be prepared. You can be assured that your character will get clobbered somewhere along the line, probably more than once when you're starting out. Most MUDs allow you to be reincarnated with the same name and description, but with fewer experience points and none of the stuff you had accumulated. If you're quick, you may be able to get your stuff from your corpse, but don't count on it. You did keep a map, didn't you?
2. Map religiously. With the size of MUDs growing all the time, and with existing MUDs expanding as players add new areas, a map is crucial if you want to succeed in the game. Go over the map tips we laid out in Chapter 2, and resist the urge to get lazy. What seems like a quick and easy path back to safety might become pretty confusing when you are badly hurt and being hunted by a mob.

3. Do not try to kill other players unless it is specifically permitted on the MUD. If you aren't sure, try using the news or info commands to find out. If all else fails, ask someone. Nothing can get you kicked off a MUD faster than slaughtering your fellow players when player killing is expressly forbidden. Check before you knock someone out.
4. Make sure to check all the news, info and help when you begin playing a new MUD. While you can usually expect the same features from MUD to MUD (especially MUDs of the same type), each MUD is different, and you can avoid hard feelings later on by making sure you know the rules before you start.
5. Use common sense when interacting with other players. Remember that there's a person on the other end of the line. If someone obviously doesn't want to be bothered, don't bother him or her. By the same token, if someone asks you for help, remember what it was like when you were a newbie and toss a few coins. Common courtesy makes the virtual road a lot smoother.
6. While this may seem like contrary advice after the last tip, it's not. Don't jump into a fight unless you are specifically asked by the player doing the fighting. Even though it may seem like a neighborly gesture, you may end up stealing all the experience points if you strike the final blow.
7. Don't loot the bodies of dead players unless it's permitted by the game. It's bad manners and can get you booted off pretty quickly. Besides, it's just ghoulish.
8. Avoid irritating other players by using the system-wide communication commands like shout, auction and gossip only when you need to.

9. Take notes while you are playing, and keep log files if possible. You can make notes in the margins of your map as you go along. If you keep logs of your MUDding sessions, you can go back and check what you did off-line in order to improve your game later.
10. Try to save your money. Most MUDs don't save your equipment when you quit, but they will save your cash. You can save your equipment on some MUDs by renting a room at an inn. This costs money. Try to maintain enough in reserve so that you can rest up at a friendly inn at the end of a long day of adventuring.
11. Read everything—often, clues are hidden deep within a benign description. Take your time and don't gallop through the game on a headlong rush to fame and fortune. The MUD was there today and will probably be there tomorrow. Take your time.
12. Respect the MUD you are playing on. Follow the rules. If the MUD is concerned with role-playing, stay in character and take your discussions of current events to IRC. If the MUD is a social MUD, don't go around trying to kill people—you won't make many friends. Basically, MUDs are run by dedicated, unpaid people who have given you the privilege of playing on their machine. Respect them, or they'll kick you off.
13. Above all, remember it's just a game. Don't sacrifice your job or your schoolwork. Do you think that after you graduate, you can brush off that 0.5 GPA by telling a prospective employer that sure, your grades stink, but you were a 32 level Wizard on The Crystal Bondage Palace of Death MUD? I don't think so. Have fun and take your MUD in moderation.

Moving On

If you've finished this chapter, congratulations! You're ready for anything that might come your way as a newbie! It may seem like a lot of information to have to absorb just to be able to play a game, but most of it boils down to two things: common sense and the ability to use the help command. With two things mastered, you're ready to conquer anything.

In the next chapter, we'll move beyond games and into the realm of virtual communities. We'll look at how these worlds differ from the MUDs. We'll also examine how MOOs, MUCKs and MUSHes were developed as an answer to some of the limitations of MUDs. We'll also examine some of the basic commands for establishing yourself, getting around and interacting with other players on a virtual community. Finally, we'll roll up our sleeves and get down to some real MOO programming when we create a real virtual home, complete with furnishings!

So if you're ready, let's press on. There's a heck of a lot more to come.

5

VIRTUAL COMMUNITIES: MOOS, MUCKS & MUSHES

What do you do if you aren't into games or have too much stress in your life to spend your off hours fighting monsters and solving quests? What if you just want to hang out and meet other people? What if you want to build your own world and stake out your own little corner of cyberspace? The place for you is in a MOO.

So, what's a MOO? MOOs are virtual communities, online worlds where socializing is more important than game playing. MOOs (and MUCKs and MUSHes) usually aren't concerned with getting points and keeping score. Instead, they are virtual realities where people can meet and hang out together. Additionally, players can add to the MOO by using a built-in programming language that allows them to create their own objects and places on the MOO. MOO characters can build "rooms" where people can visit, "things" that people can use or robots or "bots" that carry out their commands even when they aren't there.

For the sake of keeping things straight, we'll call all MOOs, MUCKs and MUSHes "virtual communities." While there are many differences among these online worlds, they all share two features: an emphasis on social interaction and an internal programming language that lets real people add virtual "things" to them.

Virtual communities are fun places, but they also can be pretty scary for newbies visiting for the first time. Never fear! This chapter is here to hold you by the hand and walk you through your first steps to becoming a full-fledged member of one of these online worlds. After a quick history lesson, we'll take a broad (and sadly over-generalized) look at the different types of virtual communities you may bump into on the Net. Next, we'll learn commands to start you walking and talking and try out some MOO programming as we build a home on a MOO. Finally, after some tips for becoming a useful member of MOO society, we'll take a peek into that hazy and exciting place where online life and real life meet. It sounds like a lot, but we'll try to get through it together and in one piece. Ready?

History of the Virtual World, Part 2

Maybe you'll get a better idea about what you can expect from these virtual communities if we step back and look at their origins. If you remember from our virtual world history lesson in Chapter 1, the first widely known online community was AberMUD, the granddaddy of online worlds. Shortly after the release of AberMUD, LPMud and DikuMUD were released. These programs improved the social aspects of online worlds. LPMud was a big step forward in MUD technology because it allowed certain players to use a sophisticated programming language called LPC to add places, objects and monsters to the MUD. For the first time, people who didn't have complete access to the MUD could add to it, allowing these virtual worlds to expand and grow in popularity. Unfortunately, the LPC programming language was based on the C programming language and was quite daunting for beginners to learn and use. Also, because people who knew the programming language could make changes to the MUD, access was limited to a few select wizards who had proven their programming ability.

Soon after the release of LPMud, Jim Aspnes released his TinyMUD to the Internet. Much smaller than existing MUD programs, TinyMUD introduced a system that allowed players to get around and build things without a complicated programming language. Because its programming language allowed most players to do only simple things like building new rooms (with the @dig command), linking them to existing rooms (using @link) and creating objects (with the @create command), TinyMUD provided a safe avenue for ordinary folks who wanted to add to their online world.

The next step was taken by Stephen White, who wrote TinyMUCK to make up for some of the shortcomings of TinyMUD. Often referred to as MUCK (a play on the word MUD), TinyMUCK gave players new programming tools and the ability to jump anywhere in the world by using the @teleport command. Now this may not seem like a big deal, but teleport provided more than just convenient movement—it allowed more social interaction. People no longer had to spend half their time mapping. If you wanted to go somewhere and be with a bunch of people, @teleport took you right there.

TinyMUSH (or MUSH) moved online worlds one step further away from games and one step closer to true communities. Also derived from TinyMUD, the original MUSH was written by Larry Foard. To distance his new creation from online games, Foard coined the term Multi-User Shared Hallucination (MUSH) because he envisioned this new type of virtual world as a community, a shared space where people could experience a virtual reality that was quite different from their real lives. TinyMUSH also introduced more powerful programming commands so that players could create things called "puppets."

Unlike MUD monsters, puppets could be created by players and programmed to hold simple conversations and perform basic tasks in the way that other players might. In effect, TinyMUSH puppets were the first virtual robots!

MOOs took a major step forward when LambdaMOO opened its virtual doors in October 1990. Developed by Pavel Curtis of the Xerox Palo Alto Research Center (Xerox PARC), LambdaMOO was inspired by the creative and social aspects of the Tiny worlds. LambdaMOO shared many of TinyMUD's interaction commands, and like TinyMUD, allowed players to build rooms and objects. However, LambdaMOO's main innovation was its language—the commands that people used to build on the MOO. LambdaMOO's object-oriented language allowed people with little or no programming ability to use existing objects to build new and better ones. Now ordinary people could get together and interact and take part in the actual building of a real virtual world. The online community was born!

Object-Oriented Design

In traditional programming, if you want to create something, you have to do several things. First, you have to decide beforehand what you want to do. Then, you have to decide how you're going to do it. That done, you must tell the computer exactly which steps to take.

For example, if you want to create a thing that acts like a box, you first have to describe the physical properties of the box to the computer—its size, capacity, location and so on. You must then describe how the box operates—how it opens, if it can be picked up, if it can be locked, and so on. All of these properties and the commands that allow the object to do things are stored as a series of instructions called a *program*.

Each "object" in our simplistic programming model must have its own set of instructions to operate. If you want another box, you must write another box program. You can borrow instructions from the first box program, but you have to copy them as instructions to the new box. If you want to create a new type of box—a box that can be locked, for example—you have to borrow box instructions from your new box, use them as the basis for your new box and then add the locking instructions. As you can imagine, this process becomes tedious when you want to create a number of unique objects.

Object-oriented programming simplifies the process. In object-oriented programming, you define objects and group them into classes based on their shared characteristics. Once you define a box class, for example—to include containers with four sides, a top and a bottom—you can create new types of boxes that share those basic properties but have additional features. For example, you could create a safe by using a box and putting a lock on it.

What does this mean to your MOO life? It means that you can create lots of cool stuff without having to be an ace programmer, because the wizards of the MOO have already definined basic object types—boxes, televisions, doors, rooms, chairs—that you can use and customize. In fact, once you've proved your super-programmer status, you can even use these objects to create your own new object classes for other people to use. What might seem like an obscure programming feature is actually a neat way to give newbies a way to create objects in the virtual community.

Types of Virtual Communities

Now that you know what makes virtual communities different from MUDs, let's take a look at the different types of worlds out there in cyberspace. The powerful combination of gathering people and giving them the power to shape their world means that there are just about as many types of virtual communities populating cyberspace as there are computers to run them on. However, let's try to break them down into a few basic categories.

Hangouts

I've used the term *hangouts* to describe virtual communities that stress social interaction over building, programming, research and other more "serious" pursuits. Just like a favorite bar or coffeehouse, these places may or may not have a theme in mind, but they have evolved into friendly places where people can come, kick back and just shoot the breeze. Often of the TinyMUSH or MUCK variety, these communities don't have a heck of a lot of building and programming going on, and you usually won't find people bogged down debating the meaning of life. What you will find is an environment where you are as likely to meet someone from across the world as from across campus. Watch out, though—since these places allow you to be whomever you want to be, many have developed special rooms for those with more amorous tastes. Things may not always be what they seem to be, and that cute bunny rubbing against your leg may want more than a pat on the head...

Communities

Like "hangouts," Communities (with a capital C) are social places. The Community, however, often has a coherent purpose or theme and a coherent social structure. You'll find such real-life entities as town councils, interest groups holding regular meetings, and even online marriages and divorces between characters. While making hard-and-fast distinctions between different types of online worlds is tough, what usually sets this world apart is a feeling of togetherness. While the overriding theme can be anything from media research to a cyberpunk city of the future, you can recognize one of these worlds by the care and interest that people on the MOO have for expanding and improving it.

Learning

One of the more "useful" types of online virtual communities is the kind that brings people together to use the technology for teaching and research. There are actual online universities where you can take real classes, and other worlds where people conduct research into how people act and interact in a text-based virtual reality. The Learning and Community worlds intersect in many ways.

Role Playing

Role-playing virtual communities are a lot like MUDs. In these communities, people take on roles from literature, myths or role-playing games. There's usually a tightly controlled theme with a story line or background that describes the setting, and often a strict set of rules for creating and playing a character. In these communities, you're expected to remain IC (in character) as much as possible and to take your out-of-character discussion to rooms that are outside the main area. The purpose is to create as realistic a world as possible. When you enter a role-playing virtual community, you become someone new—anything from an ancient vampire to a space ship captain—and you never know who you'll meet in your travels.

Walking & Talking

If you've survived for more than a few minutes in your MUD adventures, you'll be right at home on a MOO, MUCK, MUSH or other virtual community. While each type has its own idiosyncracies, the commands aren't unlike those you learned in your MUD explorations. In fact, because virtual communities are social places, you'll probably discover that the commands for getting help, moving around and talking to other people are easier to master and more flexible than those you learned as a MUDder.

Before we begin, I need to warn you. If it wasn't apparent before, our history of online communities should have convinced you that there are a lot of systems out there, each with its own programming language and guidelines. It would be impossible to take you through all the systems here, so we'll limit ourselves to learning MOO commands. Since MOO is one of the newest forms of online communities, it includes many, if not all, of the features of systems that came before (namely, TinyMUD, MUCK and MUSH). If you learn on a MOO, you'll be prepared for the rest.

Into the Sprawl

We'll begin our explorations of virtual communities on The Chiba City Sprawl, a cyberpunk-themed MOO run by SenseMedia Corporation. The Sprawl is a good place to start because it allows anyone to join and has no quotas (limits on how many things you can build). If you aren't into the cyberthing, don't worry. Like most MOOs, things on The Sprawl tend to go their own unique way once people start building!

Let's log on. The Chiba City Sprawl (The Sprawl) is located at chiba.picosof.com 7777. You can use either telnet or a client to get there—connecting to a MOO (or other virtual community) is just like connecting to a MUD. Let's go!

```
<!--

Welcome to the Chiba Sprawl. The Sprawl is a public service provided by SenseMedia.
Commands:

 'connect guest' - login to a guest character
 'connect [username] [password]' - login to the specified character

|
```

Figure 5-1: *Logging onto The Sprawl.*

Once you've connected to The Sprawl, you should see the Sprawl's logon screen (see Figure 5-1).

Not very exciting, but much niftier stuff awaits! Since this is our first visit, we'll have to assume the role of "guest." Type **connect guest** to log on.

You'll see a screen full of text that you can scroll through. It's a lot to digest at once, so let's break it down into parts.

First, the MOO tells us that

Okay,... guest is in use. Logging you in as 'Redwood_Guest'

This message means that the name "guest" is already in use by someone else exploring the MOO. If the default "guest" name has already been taken, the MOO has a series of other guest names it can use to name guests coming on board. Here, we got the strange name of "Redwood_Guest." Chances are that you'll get a different "guest " name. Don't fret. You're still on as long as the MOO says you're connected, no matter how silly your name.

Following your guest name assignment, there's some legal stuff to tell you that you're responsible for what you say and do and that if you do anything particularly nasty or illegal, SenseMedia will work with the Feds to nab you. Fine. What follows in Figure 5-2 is a bit more interesting.

```
-=-=-=-=-=-=-=-=-=-=-=-=-=-=-=-=-=-=-=-=-=-=-=-=-=-=-=-=-=-=-=-=-=-=-=-=-=-
The Sprawl - Chiba City Limits
The lights of Chiba City twinkle in the south east distance. Street lights
 intermittently glow, off to the north. The smell of inexpensive liquor and
 the whine of cathode ray tubes can be heard coming out of Webster's Bar and
 URL. An ivy covered wall partially obscures your view of the almost complete
 Chiba University to the south.
Don't forget to check out the Visitor's Center.
You see a newspaper, corkboard, silvery mirror, AEROSMITH ROCKS ChibaMOO DEC
 7, and REUNION poll here.
Ismene, Balsa_Guest, Zoey, and youngman (distracted) are here.
Obvious exits: north (to 100 Chiba Blvd), down (to Webster's Bar and URL),
 west (to 100 Pico Ave), Center (to Visitor's Center), townhall (to SenseMedia
 Town Hall), and venue (to SenseMedia Virtual Venue).
|
```

Figure 5-2: *Description of the room, its objects and occupants.*

Pretty cool, huh? The first line after the divider is the name of the "room" we're in. As in a MUD, a room can be a room or field or anything else—it's a location. Here we've found ourselves at the edge of Chiba City.

Following the name of our location is a description of our surroundings (see Figure 5-2). Below that (and the note about the Visitor's Center) is a list of objects in the room. In most cases when you are exploring The Sprawl (and other virtual communities) this is pretty much the format you'll see the information about your surroundings in—location name, description and then a list of objects you can interact with. Usually you can interact only with objects listed separately from the description. The objects that we can interact with are a newspaper, a corkboard, a silvery mirror, something called AEROSMITH ROCKS ChibaMOO DEC 7 and another object called a "REUNION poll."

Following the list of objects is a list of everyone in the room with you. In this case you see

Ismene, Balsa_Guest, Zoey, and youngman (distracted) are here.

When you actually visit The Sprawl, the names will be different because you never know who's going to drop by.

When you moved around a MUD, you usually went in one of six cardinal directions: north, south, east, west, up or down. It just isn't so in a MOO. In fact, examining how movement and exits in a MOO work will give us a little insight into how MOOs are designed.

Remember that MOOs are designed and programmed to be "object oriented." This means that everything in the MOO is defined as an object. So there are no "directions" that lead out of a room, only objects called "exits" that function as connection points between different locations. If you want to go from one place to another, you go through an exit and pop into a new room.

Below the line that told you what other people were in that room with you, you'll see this:

Obvious exits: north (to 100 Chiba Blvd), down (to Webster's Bar and URL), west (to 100 Pico Ave), Center (to Visitor's Center), townhall (to SenseMedia Town Hall), and venue (to SenseMedia Virtual Venue).

OK, so "north," "down" and "west" look like something you saw in MUDs. But here, like "Center," "townhall," and "venue," they're actually exits. In a MOO, and other MOO-like virtual communities, type the name of the exit to enter it and go to the place it's connected to. In this case, we can see where the exits are leading by looking at the names of the places in parentheses. For example, if we type **north**, we'll go to Chiba Blvd. If we type **down**, we'll end up at a place called Webster's Bar and URL. You get the idea.

Let's start at the Visitor's Center. Type **center** to get going. You should now see something like Figure 5-3.

```
center
Visitor's Center
Welcome to The Sprawl Visitor's Center. The Sprawl is the World's First
 Public Access Web Server and Multi Media MOO. Publish your own WWW home
 page, put graphics and audio in your objects and rooms. Type help @request
 when you would like a character.
You see Drinking Fountain and copy machine here.
Obvious exits: out (to The Sprawl - Chiba City Limits), Deck (to The Deck),
 Restroom (to Restroom), Survey (to SenseMedia Survey), Kiosk (to Help Kiosk),
 and Library (to The Library).
|
```

Figure 5-3: *The Visitor's Center.*

Well, this sounds promising! In fact, if you're the type that likes to skip ahead in books, Chapter 7 goes into much more detail about The Sprawl's World Wide Web/MOO interface.

Let's take a closer look at some of the objects before we go anywhere else. The excitement of going to a new place may have made you thirsty, so we'll examine the water fountain. As on a MUD, we can use the look command to get more information about objects. Type **look fountain**. You should see something like this:

> **look fountain**
> **A small chrome water fountain, mounted into the wall. There is a small button on the side for turning it on.**
> **It is not turned on.**

OK, let's get a drink. Usually, a water fountain is operated by pressing a button on its side. Type **press button**:

> **press button**
> **I don't understand that.**

Hmmm...that didn't work. Maybe we need to turn on the button. Type **turn on button**:

turn on button
I don't understand that.

No dice. Let's try something else. Maybe we just need to use the button. That's it! Type **use button**:

use button
I don't understand that.

Ahhhhh! What's going on here! Why can't we get the darn thing to work? Actually, I've dragged you through this exercise to demonstrate an important point about MOOs. Remember that "object-oriented" thing? Well, objects are assigned verbs as well as properties. These describe actions that players can perform on the object. In this case, "press," "turn on " and "use" aren't verbs that the fountain object understands. How do we find out what it understands? We use the examine command. Type **examine fountain**, and you see the fountain's verb list (see Figure 5-4).

```
Drinking Fountain (aka #4698, Drinking Fountain, and fountain)
Owned by Traveller.
A small chrome water fountain, mounted into the wall. There is a small button
 on the side for turning it on.
Obvious verbs:
 push/press fountain
 drink/sip/slurp from fountain
 g*et/t*ake fountain
 d*rop/th*row fountain
 gi*ve/ha*nd fountain to <anything>
```

Figure 5-4: *Using the examine command to look up an object's verbs.*

Now we're getting somewhere! The examine command gives us a lot of information about an object. First, it tells us the name, number and aliases of the object. In this case, the name is "Drinking Fountain," the object number is #4698, and the aliases, or alternative names, are "Drinking Fountain" and "fountain." The name is the name that the object's creator gave it. The object number uniquely identifies the object to the computer maintaining the MOO. The aliases are the other names that we can use.

Next, we find out that "Drinking Fountain" is owned by someone named "Traveller." On a MOO, owning something means that you have total control over it—only you can make changes to your object.

You can also make sure that no one else can take it by "locking" it to a location from which only you can move it.

Finally, the object's description, which we've seen, is followed by the list of "obvious verbs." In this case, we see that we can:

push/press fountain
drink/sip/slurp from fountain
g*et/t*ake fountain
d*rop/th*row fountain
gi*ve/ha*nd fountain to <anything>

Aha! That was our problem with getting a drink—we weren't using the right verbs! Now let's try **press fountain**:

press fountain
You push the button on the side of the fountain. Water spouts out.

Good. Now let's take a drink. Looking at the verb list, we see that our other choice is "slurp from fountain." Sounds good—at this point you're probably ready to slurp anyway! Type **slurp from fountain**:

slurp from fountain
You take a drink from the water fountain.

That's better! If you want to try a quick experiment, try typing **sip from fountain** or **drink from fountain**. The result's the same every time. On the list of verbs, "drink, " "sip," and "slurp" are all on the same line. This means that they do the same thing. Before we leave the fountain, also notice that examine gives you a list of "obvious verbs." Do some objects have "hidden verbs?" You bet. Is there any way to find them out? You can experiment until something works or maybe cozy up to the creator and ask. Good luck.

Now that you've learned a little about getting around the MOO, why don't you get out and poke around? Since you're still a guest, you won't be able to do anything permanent, but you can get a good taste of what's in store for you. Look around the Visitor's Center, poke your head into things and try to see as much as possible. When you're done, type **@go home** to go back to the Chiba City Limits where we started.

Talking on the MOO

In your poking around, you've probably seen other people hanging out. In fact, some of them may have noticed you and greeted you with a cheery "hello." How do you talk back? Actually, it's pretty easy. On a MUD you use the say command. On a MOO it's even easier. Just type a quotation mark (") followed by what you want to say. For example, to say "hello" to people in the room, you might try typing

"Hello everyone!

You'll immediately see something like:

You say, "Hello everyone!"

Everyone else in the room will see something like:

Redwood_Guest says, "Hello everyone!"

If you want to talk to a specific person, use the whisper command to make what you say appear only on the screen of the person you are whispering to. For example, if you type the following:

whisper "I think that Blue_Guest is my mother!" to Johnny

You'll see this:

You whisper, "I think that Blue_Guest is my mother" to Johnny

And Johnny will see this:

Guest whispers, "I think that Blue_Guest is my mother!" to you.

Emoting is a term for using nonverbal communication to express yourself to other players. On MUDs, you could do this by using either the emote commands or the built-in action commands that let you do things like dance, slap, pat or kiss other players. On MOOs, emoting serves the same function, but you'll probably find it easier to use. In fact, because the emote command lets you make your character do anything you choose, you can even use them to make yourself appear to fly around the room, mutate into a horde of bunny rabbits or just give a person a hug. Emoting gives the temporary appearance that something is occuring. If you use emote to indicate that you are mutating into a bunny, your description won't actually change. Everyone in the room will see that you are "mutating into a bunny" but when everything is over with, you'll still be the same person.

How does this powerful command work? It's easy. Say you want to kiss another character named "Blue_Guest." You'd type this:

:kisses Blue_Guest

Red_Guest and everyone else in the room would then see this:

Guest kisses Blue_Guest

Say you want to make sure the MOO doesn't put a space between your name and the words of your message. That's easy, too—just use two colons instead of one. If you type this:

::'s pants are on fire

Everyone in the room sees this:

Guest's pants are on fire.

As you can imagine, the possibilities are endless. Start a food fight (type **:throws a pie at Blue_Guest**)! Morph into your favorite president (type **:morphs into Bill Clinton**)! Emoting can help you communicate much more effectively and make your conversations a lot of fun.

Command	Description	What to Type
help	Displays detailed help on any MOO command. Can be used by itself to get an index of help topics.	help <command>
say	Lets you talk to other players in the room.	say <anything> or "<anything>"
emote	Used for nonverbal communication with everyone in the room.	emote <anything> or :<anything>:
quit	Disconnects you from the MOO.	quit
@go	Teleports you to the room you specify.	@go <room number>
page	Sends a private message to another player on the MOO, no matter where the player is.	page <player name> <message>
@who	Use this command to list everyone currently on the MOO and where they're located.	@who
home	Teleports you immediately to the room you've defined as your home with the @sethome command.	home
@send	Sends mail to someone.	@send <player name>
look	Displays the description of an object, place or person.	look <object, place or person>

Table 5-1: *Top 10 MOO newbie commands.*

Registering Your Character

Now that you've had the chance to poke around and interact with people on The Sprawl, you're probably itching to ditch this lame-o Guest character and make a name for yourself. But how? On The Sprawl, you use the @register command to register a character name and get a password. However, this isn't standard procedure with other virtual communities. Some of the more open-ended places let you create a new character the first time you log on. If a world offers this capability, you'll usually see something about a create command on the log on screen. Other online communities have been designed for very specific purposes and have strict procedures for registering new characters. Try using the help or news commands to find out how to register yourself.

On The Sprawl, we need to use the @request command to ask for a new character. Unlike MUDs, picking a name for yourself on a MOO isn't nearly as important, as long as it's one you can live with. Once you've decided on a name, you need to request it by typing **@request mycharactername for myemail@address**.

Mycharactername is the name of the character you are requesting and *myemail@address* is your e-mail address. The mysterious forces that be on the MOO now jump into action, and soon (in less than a day) you'll receive information about your new character, e-mailed straight to your Internet account.

If you want to, you can look around for a little while, but if you're ready to go after requesting your character, you can type **@quit** to leave the MOO.

Your MOO Character

Once you've received your registered name and password, you can create your character. If you haven't gotten a response giving you your name and password after 24 hours or so, do not log on again and try to create a new character! Doing so just bogs down the MOO and may accomplish nothing. Send e-mail to sprawl@sensemedia.net with the name of the character you requested, and they'll try to accommodate you.

If your request goes through, you should receive e-mail with a confirmation of your character's name and password (see Figure 5-5).

You'll notice that your character's name (in this example) is "NewbieMOOer" and you've been assigned "xxxxxx" as a temporary password. Let's use this to log on for the first time as a new character.

Telnet to **chiba.picosof.com 7777** (or use your favorite client program). After The Sprawl's welcome screen comes up, type **connect NewbieMOOer xxxxxx** (using your new character name and password). If all goes well, you'll be transported to the Chiba City Limits as a full-fledged character.

Once you've entered the MOO as a full-fledged character, there are a few things that you should do. First, you need to describe yourself and assign yourself a gender. If you don't do this, all people see when they look at you is

```
From: (Guest)85@Sprawl.moo.mud.org
To: youremail@address
Subject: Your Sprawl character, NewbieMOOer
Errors-To: sprawl@sensemedia.net
X-Mail-Agent: Sprawl (165.227.31.2 7777)
Reply-To: sprawl@sensemedia.net
Status: RO

A guest connected from your.internet.account at Mon Feb 3 20:02:57 1994 PST
requested a character on Sprawl for email address youremail@address.

A character has been created, with name "NewbieMOOer" and password "xxxxxx".
(Passwords are case sensitive.)

Sprawl is at 165.227.31.2, port 7777.

Read the help if you haven't used MOO before. A tutorial available
through the @tutorial command. Try paging the character HELP if you can't
find what you need in the help system or tutorial.

A programmer's manual and various other pieces of documentation are
available via ftp from

 parcftp.xerox.com, directory /pub/MOO


Keep your password secure; do not let anyone else connect as you.
Remember, you are responsible for what your character does. If you no
longer want your character, do not give it to anyone else. You can change
your password after you connect with the @password command.

After you connect, type `help manners' in order to see the policy on the
code of conduct expected.
```

Figure 5-5: *Your MOO character confirmation arrives.*

> **You see a player who should type '@describe me as ...'.**
> **It is awake and looks alert.**

Not too cool. Nothing screams "newbie" more than a character without a description! To describe yourself, use the @describe command. Try something like this:

> **@describe me as A tall man with a bright grin and a gleam in his eye**

If you typed the command correctly, you should then see

Description set

which means that you set your description correctly. To make sure you look the way you want to look, type **look at me**. The MOO should then say

A tall man with a bright grin and a gleam in his eye
It is awake and looks alert.

You'll notice that the MOO refers to you as an "It." That's because you don't have a gender yet. Genders are important because the MOO uses your gender to generate any pronouns that refer to you. Set your gender by typing **@gender male** or whatever gender you want (male, female, neuter). You should see something like this:

Gender set to male.
Your pronouns:
he,him,his,his,himself,He,Him,His,His,Himself

This says that your gender has been set and identifies the pronouns to be used to refer to you from now on. Remember—you can be anything you want. Your gender doesn't have to match what you happen to be in real life, and your description can be whatever you want it to be. Unlike MUDs, MOOs have few guidelines here. Some people like to descibe themselves exactly as they are in real life, while others make up entirely new identities. However, try to match your description and gender to the theme of the virtual community. If you are on a MOO, MUCK or MUSH that stresses role-playing, there may be strict guidelines for describing yourself and your gender. Check the help system if you have questions.

Building a Home

Now that you've learned how to get around and have created a real character, wouldn't it be nice to have a place to call home? To have a place where you enter the MOO every time you log on, and a place you can build in just the way you want it. Want to live in a shoe box? No problem! Have you always dreamed of living in a castle in the clouds or an asteroid in outer space? Since spaces you build can be described any way you like, you can create the home of your dreams with just a little bit of effort and a lot of imagination.

To create a home, we're going to have to delve into some of the more esoteric aspects of virtual community programming. Don't worry! It's easier than it sounds. Stick around, build your dream house and you'll even learn a little about how to program a computer.

First, let's create a new room to use as your home. @dig is the basic command for creating new rooms. When you @dig a new room, you create the room itself but nothing else—no exits, no description, no objects in the room. Those come later.

Let's create a room. The first thing that a room must have is a name. You can call your room anything you want, but avoid using the names of major rooms on the MOO. Because you can't visit every single room to find out its name, a good plan is to include your character's name in the name of the room. For example, call your room "NewbieMOOer's Castle" or something to that effect. Once you've decided on the name for your room, type

@dig "The Name of Your Room"

If all went well, you should see something like this:

The Name of Your Room (#000000) created.

Your new room is now named "The Name of Your Room," and its unique object number is #000000. WRITE THIS NUMBER DOWN! I can't stress this enough! On a MOO, things can have the same names, but their object numbers are always different. You must know the object number of your room if you want to be able to ask someone to add an entrance to it or even if you want to be able to find it again.

At this point, you've created the room but you aren't in it. You need to go there if you want to add things to it. One of the neat commands available to you on a MOO is the @go command. Using it and the object number of a room, you can teleport anywhere you want to go. Let's @go to our new room by typing

@go <#your room object number>

You should see something like this:

The Name of Your Room
You see nothing special.

You're home! However, at this point it's a big empty space with no description and nothing in it. Let's spruce things up a bit. Describing the room is almost exactly like describing yourself, except you now use "here" instead of "me":

@describe here as A comfy living room, with a lovely Navaho rug on the floor, beautiful prints on the wall, and several overstuffed Naugahide recliners.

If you typed in your description correctly, the MOO should reply:

Description set.

You have a room! Don't write a long description—people won't often read the whole thing, and it just takes up space in the MOO database. Also, try not to spend a lot of time describing objects you don't plan on creating. Don't describe your room as having "The most amazing television you've ever seen" unless you plan on creating a super television for people to play with.

To look at your creation, use the look command,

look here

You should see a description of your new home:

A comfy living room, with a lovely Navaho rug on the floor, beautiful prints on the wall, and several overstuffed Naugahide recliners.

Your next step should be to officially set this room as your home by using the @sethome command. Then, every time you log onto the MOO, you'll begin your explorations from here. Type

@sethome

The MOO should respond

The Name of Your Room is your new home.

Since your new home is pretty bare, perhaps we should create a sculpture to decorate it—perhaps a 5-foot-tall rendition of Rodin's The Thinker done in port-wine cheese.

First, let's create a sculpture, beginning with an existing object. The object that we begin with is called the "parent object" and the category it belongs to is its "parent class." Parent objects are specific objects that share characteristics with other objects in their parent class. So, if we want to create an object, the first thing we need to do is to determine what kind of object it is and what parent class it belongs to.

Fortunately, the makers of the MOO have defined several simple parent classes: notes, letters, things and containers. Notes and letters can contain words, things are generic objects, and containers can be thought of as generic objects that hold stuff. Since we want to create a sculpture, and a sculpture best fits the class "thing," we need to create a "thing" called "sculpture." "Things" can be picked up, looked at, dropped or thrown, but not much else—perfect for creating a work of art!

Now to make our sculpture. When we create something, we have to specify what parent class we are basing our creation on (in this case, "things") and give our creation a name. First, type the name you want people to see in the object list for the room. Then type any names that will function as "aliases" or other names for that object. If we want to create an object that appears as "A huge sculpture made of cheese," we'd type something like this:

@create $thing named "a huge sculpture made of cheese, sculpture"

If you typed everything correctly, you should see a message like this:

You now have a huge sculpture made of cheese (aka sculpture) with object number #000000 and parent generic thing (#5).

What does all this mean? It means that you now have in your possession an object with an official name of "a huge sculpture made of cheese," which can also be known as simply "sculpture." It has a unique MOO object number of #000000, and it was based on the parent class "generic thing, " also known as object #5.

If you type in**ventory**, you'll now see that you have a huge sculpture made of cheese in your possession:

inventory
Carrying:
a huge sculpture made of cheese

Great! Now you must give it a more detailed description. Use the @describe command as you did to describe yourself and your room, this time substituting the name of the object for "me" or "here"

@describe sculpture as A very tastefully molded rendition of Rodin's The Thinker created entirely out of port-wine cheese

You should then see

Description set.

Now, to place your sculpture in your room, type

drop sculpture

Then type

look

to see it and your room in all its glory:

The Name of Your Room
A comfy living room, with a lovely Navaho rug on the floor, beautiful prints on the wall, and several overstuffed Naugahide recliners.
You see a huge sculpture made of cheese.

It might be nice now to make an exit so that you can leave without using @go or @teleport commands. First, go out and find a place to connect your home to. You can do that by typing **@go #11** to get to the Chiba City Limits. From there, explore until you find an area that you'd like to connect to. The Sprawl is organized around several streets, so keep looking until you find a fairly uninhabited one.

Once you've found the street, use the examine command to find out who "owns" that street and what its object number is. I've picked 400 Chiba Blvd. as an example (see Figure 5-6).

```
examine here

400 Chiba Blvd (aka #125 and 400 Chiba Blvd)
Owned by archrocker.
The 400 block of Chiba Blvd. A large, old, decrepit warehouse lies to the north
east. The number 406 hang loosely over the door. The area is well-lit by huge
spotlights on the roof of the warehouse; probably to make up for the street light
 which seem to have nearly all been shot out here. A concrete staircase leads
 up to an old brownstone on the west side of the street.
```

Figure 5-6: *Using the examine command.*

As you can see, the examine command gives you the name and aliases for your location, as well as its unique object number, owner and description. Write down the object number—we'll need it in a minute.

Next, go home using the home command:

home
You run all the way home.
The Name of Your Room
A comfy living room, with a lovely Navaho rug on the floor, beautiful prints on the wall, and several overstuffed Naugahide recliners.
You see a huge sculpture made of cheese.

You can create an exit by using the @dig command to tell the MOO where you'd like your exit to connect and what you'd like it to be called. Here's an example:

@dig out,o,leave to #125

In this example, we've dug an exit called "out" (also referred to as "o" or "leave") from your home to 400 Chiba Blvd., object number #125. It's important to use the object number when you're making an exit so that the MOO knows exactly where you are trying to go. If you just use the name, the MOO assumes you're creating a new location and assigns that place a new object number. Remember, in a MOO, object numbers are unique—names aren't.

If all went well, you should see a message similar to this one:

Exit from The Name of Your Room (#000000) to 400 Chiba Blvd (#125) via {"out", "o", "leave"} created with id #000000. However, I couldn't add #000000 as a legal entrance to 400 Chiba Blvd. You may have to get its owner, archrocker, to add it for you.

Whoa! What does it mean that it couldn't add your exit as a "legal entrance?" Don't worry—all that means is that all exits created between rooms owned by two different people are one-way—the person creating the exit can make the exit appear from the room they own (in this case, your home), but cannot make an exit appear in a room someone else owns. While this can be a pain, it does keep people from adding exits and entrances without the permission of the owner.

The final step to adding an exit is to send mail to the owner of the room, asking him or her to add an exit so that your room is now accessible to everyone. Sending mail on a MOO is easy but kind of strange. Let's take it step by step.

We know that the owner of 400 Chiba Blvd. is someone named "archrocker." Since we want to send this person e-mail, we must use the @send command:

@send archrocker

The MOO responds with:

Subject:
[Type a line of input or '@abort' to abort the command.]

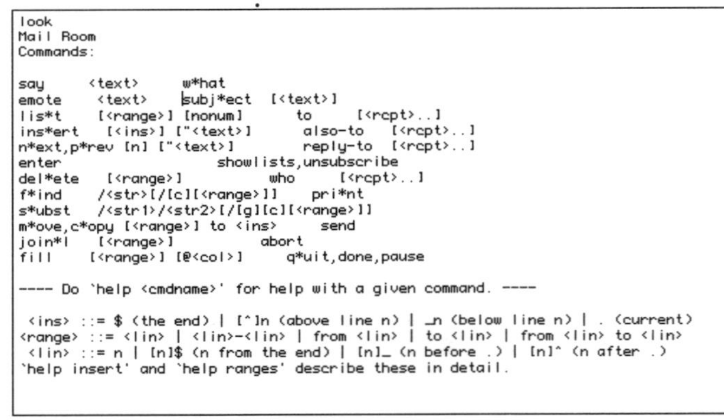

```
look
Mail Room
Commands:

say      <text>      w*hat
emote     <text>     subj*ect  [<text>]
lis*t     [<range>] [nonum]       to      [<rcpt>..]
ins*ert    [<ins>] ["<text>]       also-to    [<rcpt>..]
n*ext,p*rev [n] ["<text>]          reply-to  [<rcpt>..]
enter                        showlists,unsubscribe
del*ete    [<range>]            who      [<rcpt>..]
f*ind     /<str>[/[c][<range>]]     pri*nt
s*ubst    /<str1>/<str2>[/[g][c][<range>]]
m*ove,c*opy [<range>] to <ins>      send
join*l    [<range>]             abort
fill     [<range>] [@<col>]      q*uit,done,pause

---- Do `help <cmdname>' for help with a given command. ----

 <ins> ::= $ (the end) | [^]n (above line n) | _n (below line n) | . (current)
<range> ::= <lin> | <lin>-<lin> | from <lin> | to <lin> | from <lin> to <lin>
 <lin> ::= n | [n]$ (n from the end) | [n]_ (n before .) | [n]^ (n after .)
`help insert' and `help ranges' describe these in detail.
```

Figure 5-7: *Mail commands, as displayed from the help system.*

Type a subject for your message (in this example, type **connection request**) and press Enter (or Return):

You should then see this:

Mail Room
Do a 'look' to get the list of commands, or 'help' for assistance.
Composing a letter to archrocker (#2) entitled "Connection Request"

If you want a list of mailing commands, you can type **look** and the commands will be displayed as shown in Figure 5-7.

To get help on a specific command, type **help** and the name of the command, but really, using mail is just like speaking. To add a line to your message, just use the say command. Keep saying to add new lines. Type **send** to send your message when you're done. Your message might look something like this:

say Hi!
say I was wondering if you could add an exit from 400 Chiba Blvd.
say to my room (#000000). The number of the exit from my room
say is #000000.
say If it wouldn't be too much trouble, I'd like you to use "down"
say and "d" as words to describe your exit to my room.
say Thanks!
say NewbieMOOer
send

After you type **send**, the MOO will respond with:

Sending...
Mail actually sent to archrocker (#2)

You will be put back in your home. That's all there is to it! Hopefully, in a few days or so, you'll receive mail from the person who you sent mail to, telling you that you are connected.

Being a Useful Member of Society

Now that you've established your place on the MOO, there are things you need to know about who's running the MOO, how you fit in and how to get information about life online.

MOO Mail

One of the best ways to find out what's happening is to subscribe to some of the MOO mailing lists. Just like real-life e-mail mailing lists, these groups are discussions about various topics that are carried out through e-mail. Subscribers post messages to the list, and the messages arrive in your mailbox. You can read them, post messages of your own and participate in ongoing discussions about online life.

So, how do you get on one of these lists? First, you need to tell the MOO that you want to be on the list using the @subscribe command. Let's try it out. While you are online to The Sprawl, type @**subscribe**. You should then see something like Figure 5-8.

```
@subscribe
*NS (#288) [Public]
 Announcements and notices about new places, objects,
verbs and the like.
*Bug-Reports, *Bugs, *Bug (#341) [Public]
 The obvious.
*social-discussion, *s, *soc, *si (#560) [Public]
 A mailing list for the discussion of social issues on
this MOO. Please refrain from flaming.
*wizards-r-us (#741)
 Self-explanatory. Try not to mail progbit-requests
here, try to find someone online.
*WOW, *W (#909) [Public]
 A list for anything you think would fit. Totally obvi-
ous statements by friends, or things that just don't
really make sense but have an aire of authority.
*projects, *p, *pro, *proj (#1117) [Public]
 Please announce major projects and plans here. This is
to help our Chiba-brothers and Chiba-sisters from wast-
ing time doing the same things others are doing, as well
as a place to seek help and/or suggestions for new
projects before formally announcing them on *New Stuff.
*qooc, *q (#1850) [Public]
 Quoted Out Of Context - No whining!
*WWW, *Web (#1303) [Public]
 This can either be a mailing list or a mail folder,
depending on what mood you're in...
```

```
*Museum (#2989) [Public]
 This is a mailbox for the Oasis Hotel residents (400
Nano) for future building plans, topography discussion,
and whatever else anyone has to say. Feel welcome to
join the fray:)
*Programming, *prog (#5454) [Public]
 Programming questions/answers.
*journal (#4125) [Public]
 List to send anonymous messages about sensitive topics
to make you and perhaps someone else feel better. The
anonymity frees you to discuss topics of a personal
nature. Please do not discuss other people or criticize
a post on this list. Messages to this list are, by de-
fault, anonymous. To send an attributed message, include
the line "attributed" somewhere in the body
*RPG-Development (#9275) [Public]
 Pretty much what it says folks. This mailing list is
for people who are interested in RPG and have ideas for
it's development, or would like to help in its growth.
*Metaverse (#9450) [Public]
 The kewlest mailing list for talking about the
Metaverse, and its creation.
*theme (#9961) [Public]
 List for theme-related discussion
*Topography (#10032) [Public]
 Sprawl Topography Discussions
*Space (#6109) [Public]
 This can either be a mailing list or a mail folder,
depending on what mood you're in... this is a newsletter
to discuss the development of space here on the sprawl.
Including space lanes, RPG development, and Space sta-
tion development.
*style, *advice (#12759) [Readable]
 A list to discuss programming style, design, testing,
and other lofty programming topics.
```

```
*Music (#4181) [Public]
 This is a mailing/discussion list for Music. The pur-
pose of this list is so that underground/noncommercial
bands/labels may networrok. I would prefer if you re-
viewed the bands you post <give a description, etc...>.
Please do not post about major bands <unless you're
reviewing>, we all know these already. I will continu-
ally post new music since I work in radio. Help your
local bands!
—— end of @subscribe ——
```

Figure 5-8: *MOO mailing lists.*

As you can see, there's a lot to talk about! Each line beginning with an asterisk (*) gives the name of a new mailing list, as well as the aliases you can use to refer to the list. For example, the first list that you see is the New Stuff list:

***NS (#288) [Public]**
Announcements and notices about new places, objects, verbs and the like.

Officially, it's referred to by its initials, NS. The number following the name of the list is our old friend, the object number, which defines the list to the MOO computer. *[Public]* indicates that *NS is a public mailing list—anyone can subscribe to it, read it and post new messages to it. The next line gives the description, which tells us the list a good place to learn about new objects and places that have been created as well as any other new stuff on the MOO.

So, let's subscribe to *NS:

@subscribe *NS

You should then see a message like this:

New Stuff (#288) has 335 messages. You will be notified immediately when new messages are posted.

Now we're on the New Stuff list. When people post new messages to the list, you'll get a message right away (provided that you're online) telling you that a new message has been posted to the list.

If you want to subscribe to more mailing lists, just follow the same procedure, substituting the new list name after the @subscribe command.

Next, to see what messages are already on the list, use the @rn command. This command not only tells you what mailing lists you have subscribed to, but it also tells you how many messages are waiting to be read. Type **@rn** to try it out. You should see something similar to this:

@rn
There is new activity on the following lists:
New Stuff (#288) 335 new messages

This tells us that we've subscribed to one mailing list (New Stuff) and that there are 355 messages waiting to be read. Let's start by reading the first message. Messages on mailing lists are identified by their number, so type

@read 1 on *NS

Figure 5-9 shows what a MOO mailing list message looks like.

If you want to read other messages on the list, just use the @read command in the same way, putting in the number of the message that you want to read. Once you get tired of reading new messages, you can mark the entire list as "read" (meaning that @rn won't show it as containing any new messages) by using the @read last on *NS command. This command shows you the last message posted to the list and mark every other message as "read" by you.

```
@read 1 on *NS
Message 1 on New Stuff (#288):
Date:   Tue Jun 14 23:38:14 1994 PDT
From:   Stetson (#204)
To:    *New Stuff (#288)
Subject: New list

Well, we have a pretty new list here, and we're doing new stuff all the time, so
 I created this list to try to keep track of it all. Use this list to send annou
ncements of new features, verbs, $player features, Feature Objects, Generic Pare
nts, geographic expansion, whatever.
Have a blast!

-Stetson-
--------------------------
|
```

Figure 5-9: *Reading message 1.*

What if you want to post a message to the list? It's as easy as sending mail to another player. Let's say you've created a home you're really proud of and you want to invite people over. To announce your open house, you want to post a message to the New Stuff list. You'll use the @send command, but this time use the name of the list rather than a person as the address:

@send *NS

Just like when you sent mail before, the MOO will prompt you for a subject:

Subject:
[Type a line of input or '@abort' to abort the command.]

Type something like **NewbieMOOer's Open House**! and press Enter (or Return). You'll be placed in the Mail room where you use the say command (or ") to type each line of your message, the send command to send it off, and quit to leave the mail room:

Once you've finished your message, type send and then quit to transmit your announcement to the mailing list. If the message has been sent successfully, you'll see a confirmation (see Figure 5-10).

```
say NewbieMOOer would like to announce an open house on
say Saturday, December 5 at 5:30pm EST. Come see this new addition
say to The Sprawl. NewbieMOOer will be there to answer questions
say and chat. You can also see his latest creation: Rodin's The Thinker
say stunningly sculpted in port-wine cheese!
say You can get to my house by @go ing to #000000.
say I'm looking forward to seeing you!
say -------------
say NewbieMOOer
send
quit
```

Figure 5-10: *Announcing your new home.*

Your message is in transit.
Mail actually sent to New Stuff (#288)
New Stuff (#288) has just been sent new mail by NewbieMOOer (#0000).

It's as easy as that! Once you send your message and quit the mail room, your words go out to everyone else on the New Stuff mailing list. Since you're on the mailing list, you are notified that a new message (YOUR message!) has been added to the list.

The MOO mail system is a great way to stay in touch with other people on the MOO and to find out about new places, things, meetings and events. We've only scratched the surface. Use the help mail command to explore your many options. If you're on another type of virtual world, look into the mail system there. Check help or news to find out more about using them. Staying in touch is an important part of building online community.

Online Meetings, Lectures & Discussions

When you set up your open house, you did something many other people do on a MOO—you held a scheduled appearance. People from all over the world often meet on a MOO as a way of holding lectures, organized discussions or meetings that never would really be possible outside of a MOO. If fact, it's not uncommon for people to upload the text of papers that they have written as a "lecture" and then invite discussion afterwards in virtual question-and-answer sessions. Budding fiction and poetry writers often hold scheduled "readings" of their work. The possibilities are endless! You can find out about these virtual events by checking the mailing lists, talking to other players, or reading bulletin boards and other public messages.

Moving On

If you've followed along so far, congratulations! You're not a newbie anymore! We've been through a lot together, from your first steps out into the Internet with telnet all the way up to programming your first MOO room. I'm so (snif!) proud of you!

However, even though you may know all the technical stuff about navigating through virtual worlds, there's one part of your education that we haven't covered yet—MUDetiquette. Virtual worlds are social places, and how you conduct yourself online is just as important as how many monsters you kill or how many neat objects you can program. So, if you're ready, it's time to take a whirlwind look at MUD (and MOO) manners.

6

ONLINE ETIQUETTE

Sometimes even the best intentions can get you into a heap of trouble. Even though we may try to conduct ourselves with the utmost aplomb, manners are tricky. What might pass as good behavior in one place can be considered a hideous breach of etiquette somewhere else. Your life online is no exception.

I consider myself a polite person—I hold the door open for people, I've mastered the correct fork usage and I usually don't wipe my hands on the dog when he walks by the table. You'd think that someone with my impeccable manners would have no problem conducting himself online. Well, not quite...

One night, I was exploring a MUD—just poking around and doing a bit of exploring. Nothing much was happening and I was itching for a bit of adventure, so when I rounded a corner and saw a fight, I rushed over to see what was going on.

I could see right away that a fellow MUDder was getting pummeled by a monster and seemed inches away from certain death. Thinking I was doing the right thing, I leaped into the fray and with a few swift blows I vanquished the monster and saved the stranger. I stepped back to bask in the glow of my good deed, ready to accept the praise I knew I had coming to me. It didn't take long.

"You as***e!" he yelled, "You got all my experience points!"

"Uh, sorry," I responded, "I thought I'd help you out."

"Jerk," he spat as he stomped away, "If I ever see you again, I'll kill you."

I was confused. I thought that I had done the right thing by stepping in and helping. It slowly dawned on me that by striking the final blow, I had "stolen" all the experience points he was due. I had just learned my first lesson in MUD etiquette: Ask before you leap.

Emily Post Goes Online

Most people are online to have fun, not to be stifled by some complex set of rules that no one can remember or understand. Following proper online etiquette doesn't have to feel like a childhood visit with your stuffy Aunt Mabel. Understanding online etiquette is simple: Follow the rules of the game, don't do anything you wouldn't do in real life and use common sense. Newbies often get into trouble because they don't take into account the unique ways of online life. Instead, they go charging around, doing whatever comes to mind and generally aggravating everyone around them. This doesn't have to happen to you. Even though each online world may have its own specific rules of behavior, there are certain universal guidelines. Read on to find out what they are.

Building Online Community

No matter what type of online world you enter, always remember that you're not alone—there's always a real person on the other end of the line. In fact, meeting new people and making new friends online is what makes exploring these virtual worlds so interesting. It's pretty easy, however, to forget that those glowing letters on your screen represent another person. Most online misunderstandings occur when people act in ways that they never would in real life because they can't see the other person. This isn't a phenomenon that's unique to MUDs, either. Internet newsgroups are often choked by flamewars that erupt when people, using the distance that the keyboard allows, speak to other people in ways that they probably wouldn't dream of in their personal contact with people.

This isn't to say that you have to always behave online as you would in the real world. Virtual worlds are interesting because they give people with ordinary lives the opportunity to become someone new. Meek, mild-mannered people who wouldn't dream of hurting a fly in real life can become vicious, ruthless killers, while tough corporate raiders sometimes relax by taking on the persona of a woodland creature and frolicking through a virtual forest. Online you may do things that you wouldn't do in real life—propositioning a stranger, assassinating an enemy, rifling through someone else's house without their permission—but it's important that you always act in the context of the community you're visiting. If you're on a player-killing, no-holds-barred MUD (like Games of Death), you can go around wiping out whomever you want because that's one of the things people on that MUD expect. On the other hand, if you go hunting in a place like FurryMUCK where people take the forms of animals and romp in a peaceful forest wonderland, you'll be sure to ruffle a few feathers and get kicked off. The whole idea is that as a member and player in a virtual world you are a member of a real, live community with its own rules and customs. Building community by staying within the guidelines is an important part of any world, game or not.

Different Worlds, Different Ways

Like I've said before, different worlds mean different ways. MUDs, MOOs, MUSHes, MUCKs and TinyMUDs all allow people to interact differently and to varying degrees, and all have their own special forms of etiquette. However, we can simplify online etiquette by dividing it into two categories: MUDiquette and virtual community etiquette.

MUDiquette

MUDs are games, and conducting yourself with aplomb on a MUD has a lot to do with your ability to follow the rules of the game. Some of these rules are written, some are not. When you log onto a MUD for the first time, it's best to learn the rules of the game—many MUDs aren't too coy about booting misbehaving characters off the MUD and banning them from ever returning. So, to avoid future embarrassment (or banishment) it's a good idea to type **help rules** or **info policy** or something similar to see what the rules of the MUD are.

These commands may yield you pages and pages of MUD rules and regulations, or at the very least some general guidelines for you to follow.

If these commands don't give you enough information, you may want to try the news or info command. If all your attempts at finding some written rules fail, talk to other players to find out what, if any, guidelines you're expected to follow on the MUD. Figure 6-1 shows InfinityMUD's Policy statement.

```
 ______________________________.oOo.___________________________
/                                                              \
|                         InfinityMUD Policy                    |
|______________________________________________________________|
Last Updated: Nov 10th 1994

O__________Overview:

This MUD is now being run under the supervision of the New
Mexico Tech computer center, and is also the on-line Virtual
world for the Virtual World Club of New Mexico Tech. Because
of this, we are trying to make this a kinder, more tame,
toned-down MUD.

O__________Bug Discoveries:

If you discover a bug in the game, of any type, please report
it by using the "Bug" command, or telling the Gods. If find a
bug, abuse it to your advantage, and don't report it, then you
aren't positively contributing to the MUD, and this will be
frowned upon.

O__________Deathroom Recoveries:

Deathroom recoveries will no longer be possible. If you hit a
deathroom, your stuff will be automatically destroyed (pit-
ted). Depending on what level you are, you may get your points
back, or not lose your stuff at all. Wizards may not resurrect
items from the pit. While we do not mean to appear cruel or
unusual, the purpose of deathrooms is to cause you grief by
nuking your equipment and kicking you off the game.

O__________Lag-Death Re-Frobs:

Wimpy mode (automatic flee at a certain strength) has been
implemented, so no lag-death refrobs will be given out. This
eliminates the hassle of trying to determine the validity of
such requests and gives players the control of how well they
are safeguarded against lagdeath.
```

O__________Heals:

It is perfectly acceptable to ask for a heal. However, no one is REQUIRED to heal you, so don't WHINE if you don't get one. Also, wizards may only HEALALL, this is to preserve fairness when heals are given out. Prophet+ have the HEAL command as well as HEALALL. Wizards: If we think you are healing too much, you may lose your heal p-flag.

O__________Cheating:

Cheating will not be tolerated. In most cases, the way you've found to cheat will be discovered, and then "programmed out." However, cheating, such as killing your link in a fight or "passing out stuff" as a wizard will result in penalty assessment.

O__________Cursing:

Occasional "brief" cursing will be overlooked, but players intentionally cursing at other players or repeatedly cursing will probably suffer the penalties.

O__________Harassment:

Harassment will not be tolerated. If you are harassing somebody with repeated tells, echo's, echoto's, shouts, chats, etc. - you will suffer the penalties.

O__________Exorcisms/Time-Outs:

If you are kicked off the game for any reason, it's a good idea to quit what you were doing, just be quiet, and don't do it again. After all, is it that big of a deal that you have to reconnect? No. Is it a big deal to have to run to wizard again? Yes.

```
O__________Inhabitation of Wizards:

It is now our official stance that any wizard character which
is connected to the game must be inhabited by whoever ran it
to wiz. This precludes the validity of giving away 'spare'
wizard characters. We will probably tolerate most already-
existing situations where people have been given wizards which
were either run by someone else or simply frobbed up, but we'd
really like to see any new wizards on the game be completely
valid.

O__________Running other Characters:

You are allowed to run other characters (that you intend to
play yourself) to wizard. However, they must be YOUR charac-
ters. You may not run other players' characters to wizard at
any time. Please note it is quite unfair to other players to
be running more than one character at the same time (both in
the game at once), so this will be highly discouraged.

O__________The BECOME Command:

It has always been considered cheating to use your own wizard
character to help your mortal character, and this is *espe-
cially* true when you become back and forth between the two.
This is very unfair to other mortals, whether they have wizard
characters or not, and it will not be tolerated if it is
observed. If you have been using these sorts of methods,
please discontinue them. We may consider putting restrictions
on the become command if this becomes (haha) more of a prob-
lem, so please use it wisely.

O__________Macros:

Please use macros sparsely and with care. As always, it is in
your best interest to treat fellow runners fairly and with
courtesy. This means it isn't cool to use running pattern
macros (macros which when executed will run you through a
```

```
pattern of gathering key items or moving through zones) unless
you're the only mortal on. If you know the pattern you can
type it in yourself and thus give other mortals a fair shake
(as well as change your mind in the middle of the run). If you
don't know the pattern you have no business using someone
else's knowledge to give you an edge over other runners, and
you'll probably end up getting lost anyway. Be aware that the
uppers have the power to enforce this at their discretion and
apply whatever penalties they see fit.

o__________Penalties:

If you break any of the above policy:
1st offense: You will be warned and possibly kicked off the
game. 2nd offense: You will be kicked off again and/or the
game will be locked. 3rd offense: You could be zapped (utterly
destroyed).

o__________General Comments:

We are not trying to emphasize strictness and punishment
themes here, although we expect players to be mature enough to
handle them. We want this MUD to be a little more "toned down"
than the last time it was run.

              /*-PLEASE NOTE-*\
The Gods reserve the right to enforce & change the policy as
they see fit.
```

Figure 6-1: *InfinityMUD's (129.138.4.119 6715) Policy statement.*

As you can see, this is a pretty comprehensive list, covering just about any gaffe you could make on this MUD. While this statement is unique to one MUD, it's indicative of the kinds of rules that apply to a lot of other MUDs. In fact, many standards of behavior are universal. Let's take a look at a few of them.

Shouting

One of the more obnoxious and annoying things you can do on a MUD is abuse the shout, holler or yell commands. These commands are generally used to broadcast your words to everyone else on the MUD. Some MUDs might use different commands to accomplish the same thing, but you'll find that just about every online world has them in some form. Why can shouting be a problem? First of all, there's often a lot going on when you're MUDding, and lots of stuff scrolling up the screen. Even if you use a client, trying to keep track of all the words coming at you can get pretty confusing, especially if you are having a group conversation or are in the middle of fighting a monster. When someone shouts, their words show up on your screen along with everything else, often with confusing results. Shouts can be particularly annoying if you use telnet to connect to a MUD, because you'll often find that people's shouts get mixed in with what you're trying to type or read.

This isn't to say that there aren't legitimate uses for shout—there are. However, using it to broadcast that someone you don't like is an idiot or that you've just reached a new level isn't necessary. In fact, most people probably don't care. If you need to talk to people all over the MUD at once, you may want to check to see if you have access to channels where you can selectively tune in or turn off other conversations. Also, some MUDs have specialty broadcast commands like auction that allow you to broadcast to other people on the MUD for specific reasons—auctioning off unneeded equipment, for example.

Language

Using appropriate language is important on most MUDs. Of course, everyone's interpretation of what is "appropriate" differs, and each MUD might have its own policies on how salty your language can be, but there are certain words you can be pretty sure you won't be allowed to use. Words like...well, I can't even use them here, but you know the four-letter varieties that probably apply. As with any community, standards of language vary from the strictly professional to the lewd, but you're probably safe most of the time if you stick to words that your mother would deem appropriate for "mixed company." Strong language might add spice every now and then, but you're probably safest sticking to blander forms of expression until you've been on the MUD for a while.

Harassment

Defining what constitutes harassment can be difficult, but usually it means persisting to bother someone even after they've told you to stop. The definition of "bother" varies from MUD to MUD, and on a MUD where you're allowed to kill other players, pummeling another player into cyberdust usually isn't defined as "bothering" them. However, no matter where you go, making a pest of yourself is bad form. If you go up and start a conversation with someone and they tell you to leave, then leave. Continuing to talk with someone who doesn't want to be bothered not only makes you look like a twit, but it can be pretty annoying for everyone.

Sexual harassment on a MUD can be a touchy subject (see the sidebar on cyber-rape). While some MUDs are devoted to "TinySex"—simulated sexual activity in a MUD setting—the best approach is never to assume that making sexual advances on other players, unless you've read it in the MUD guidelines

Cyber-rape One of the most destructive and most publicized breaches of MOO etiquette occurred in March 1993 on LambdaMOO. In fact, the event caused so much of a stir that Julian Dibbell wrote a fairly lengthy article about it for the *Village Voice.*

What happened has been described as everything from a rape to a harmless prank, and the fact that the event took place on an online virtual reality makes it even harder to examine. Perhaps the facts should speak for themselves. On a Monday night in March of 1993, in the communal space known as the "Living Room" on LambdaMOO, a character named Mr. Bungle appeared. He wasn't a pretty sight—he described himself as "a Bisquick-faced clown dressed in [deleted] stained harlequin garb and girdled with a mistletoe-and-hemlock belt" bearing an obscene inscription. His appearance was bad enough, but what he did next sent shock waves through the MOO community.

Mr. Bungle had created several "voodoo dolls," puppets controlled by him that appeared to be real characters on the MOO. By manipulating these dolls though MOO commands, Mr. Bungle created a scene in which characters appeared to be doing his bidding. Using his voodoo dolls, he first forced legba, one of the more well-known characters on the MOO, to have sex with him. At first, the people in the room didn't know how to react, but they got their wits together and firmly ejected him from the room. However, because he could operate his dolls from anywhere on the MOO, he stayed in his home room and proceeded to violate other characters in the Living Room. This continued until another, more powerful character was able to disable him.

What followed the attack shook the roots of the LambdaMOO community. Some characters immediately began petitioning for Mr. Bungle's total annihilation. Others wanted him "toaded"—his characteristics and description wiped and replaced with the attributes of a toad. Some people argued that what he did was a harmless prank, and that ignoring him was the best punishment. Eventually, after much debate, Mr. Bungle was summoned for a public hearing where he confronted those he had violated. Unrepentant to the last, Mr. Bungle tried to make a case for himself as one who was just experimenting with the social implications of virtual reality. Ultimately, JoeFeedback, one of the wizards of the MOO, acted alone and deleted his character. Mr. Bungle was dead.

→

or have had several reputable players tell you it's OK. No matter what's the case, the best approach is not to make a move on another player unless you've established enough rapport with the person to be able to tell if you think they might be interested. Showing up in a crowed living room, dropping your virtual pants and yelling "Hey hot mommas, come and get some lovin!" is just as inappropriate on a MUD as it is in real life. Also, don't be too quick to jump into the virtual sack if someone seems over-eager to initiate an erotic encounter with you. Since you can be anyone (and anything) you want to be in a text-based virtual reality, sometimes things aren't what they seem. In fact, some people get their jollies by coercing an unsuspecting partner into a MUD sex encounter, capturing the whole thing, and uploading it to the Internet. You can probably imagine how embarrassing that could be.

Playerkilling

After sex, playerkilling is probably the second touchiest MUDiquette topic. Playerkilling is just what it says—slaying other characters on a MUD.

Playerkilling can take many forms—ambushing unsuspecting players, killing them in a head-to-head fight or finding other people to help you kill a certain character. However, the result is still the same—the character is wiped out and has to be built up again from scratch. People tend to get very attached to their characters, and wiping out someone just because you happen to be stronger than they are can cause hard feelings that never go away. Even though someone may have something you want, unless a MUD specifically allows playerkilling, don't try it! On most MUDs that don't allow playerkilling, it's usually grounds for immediate expulsion.

There are some MUDs where playerkilling is allowed, but even on these MUDs, the killing of other players is usually governed by some set of rules. On some MUDs, you can only kill players in prearranged "tournament" matches where characters can battle it out to the death. On other MUDs, playerkilling is limited to certain parts of the MUD or only allowed during certain times. If the MUD guidelines specifically state that playerkilling is allowed, then go for it—it's part of the gory fun of MUDding. However, even on playerkilling MUDs, it's considered bad form to take out your frustrations by going around and wiping out newbies for sport. Not only do you look like a jerk, but you always need to remember that the newbie you wiped the floor with today may be a wizard tomorrow. Use common sense.

As horrifying as his acts were, Mr. Bungle's behavior accomplished something—what had previously been merely thought of as a fun diversion had become a community, and that LambdaMOO's members had to make decisions and support each other as a community. Mr. Bungle hasn't returned, but the legacy of his actions lives on—what we do online can inspire feelings just as real and just as strong as what we do in real life.

Helping

So you're a nice human, with love in your heart and malice toward no one. You know in your heart that killing other players is wrong and you decide to make it your life's work to wander around the MUD like the Lone Ranger, a bright paragon of justice who spends his or her time helping others in their fights. This may be a noble (by sappy) ideal, but it's just as sure to get you into trouble as being an indiscriminate killer. Why? You saw what happened to me at the beginning of this chapter. After a battle, MUDs usually award experience points to the person who actually killed the monster—the person who struck the last blow.

If you happen to see someone in a pitched battle and you stride over and wipe out the weakened monster they've been fighting for the last half hour, you'll be the one to get all the experience points that they would have received if they had killed the monster. People tend to get a little miffed if this happens. If you encounter someone fighting a monster, ask before you jump in. If you insist on being the caped crusader of the MUD, check the MUD help system to see if the MUD you are on has an assist command. This command makes sure that the spoils of a fight are distributed equitably. Other MUDs have band or group commands that accomplish the same thing.

Hinting

Just as irritating and unwanted as serial do-gooders are people who go around telling other people how to solve puzzles and MUD quests. It's usually considered bad form to give away hints because, after all, MUDs are games, and solving puzzles and succeeding in quests are an important part of that game. Giving away the answers not only irritates all the other people who lost sleep and study time solving a particularly difficult riddle, but it also ruins the game for the person you're helping. Half the fun of MUDding is solving puzzles, and as far as reality goes, a sense of accomplishment is really your only reward.

Your judgment is the only guideline you have to determine what's a hint and what's an answer. There's a fine line between giving a little nudge and giving away the whole enchilada. As an example, if you know that a puzzle can only be solved by giving a green stone to the giant and you tell someone "give the green stone to the giant" then you can be pretty sure that you're giving it away. On the other hand, telling them that they "probably should consider what a monster needs" to solve their quest is probably within the "helpful" range. With experience, you'll get better at giving hints. In the meantime, try to keep your mouth shut.

Multiple Characters

Because of the way the Internet works, it's possible to have multiple connections from your account to a MUD. At first this might seem like a really great way to be your own best friend—you can explore two places at the same time or have two characters to gang up on monsters. Technically, there's really not much the owners of a MUD can do to prevent you from having multiple connections, but you can bet the farm that you'll be kicked off most MUDs if they find out. Why is this such a horrible thing? Well, not only is it cheating, but the additional connections slow down the MUD and cause the dreaded phenomenon called "lag." Don't do it.

Exploiting Bugs

During your MUDding adventures, chances are you'll find a bug in the system that allows you to do things you probably shouldn't be able to do. Perhaps it's a flaw in the program or maybe it's a setting that shouldn't be set. Either way, exploiting bugs in the program to get an unfair advantage is usually grounds for dismissal from the MUD. No one's going to kick you off if you find a bug by mistake and it helps you out. However, if you keep using it and don't report it to the MUD wizards (using the bug command), you'll probably get in big trouble. Exploiting bugs to gain an unfair advantage also has a another name: cheating.

You can probably tell by now that most of the stuff that passes for MUD etiquette is good judgment and common courtesy. It's the basic stuff that you (hopefully!) learned in kindergarten, but you'd be surprised how many people become five-year-olds again when online. These rules don't and can't possibly cover every situation that you might encounter during your MUDding career and if you're even half as devious as I think you are, you'll probably be able to think up even sneakier ways to cheat. Resist that temptation—MUDs that are fair and fun should stay that way.

Etiquette in the Virtual Community

Because most virtual communities aren't as gamelike as MUDs, they tend to be a little looser when it comes to rules and etiquette. You usually won't find a set of written rules for behavior, and the owners of the community aren't as visible as they are on a MUD. In most of these places, the people running the world often try to stay as far in the background as possible, preferring to let the community govern itself. This hands-off policy usually results in more liberal codes of conduct than what you'd find on a MUD, but it also can mean some pretty interesting interactions.

As many online worlds approach a state of cooperative anarchy, however, there's usually some standards of behavior that apply no matter where you are. These general guidelines may not apply to every situation, but they're good rules to live by until you've gotten your bearings. Let's check them out.

Interactions

On a virtual community, your behavior, interactions with other players and even your building and description should take into account the overall theme of the world. If you are on a role-playing world, there are often strict guidelines you must adhere to, the least of which is to stay IC (in character) as much as possible. Role-playing worlds are designed as places where you leave your real-life persona behind and become someone else, with that person's speech habits, personal code of conduct and appearance. Role-playing worlds are usually so adamant about this that you can't even get an account on one without first submitting a character profile to the owners of the world. Once online, assume the behaviors of your new character and stay within the theme of the world.

Building Codes

One of the features that sets virtual communities apart from your typical game-playing MUDs is your ability to add rooms and objects to that world. Building interesting objects is as much an art as it is a skill, but taking care to design interesting and non-confusing spaces is something to strive for.

Some simple guidelines that I've paraphrased from the MediaMOO's building code are:

1. Building one room is better than building two. Don't spread your design talents thin by creating a bunch of boring spaces when you could build one interesting room.
2. Provide exits for your rooms. Nothing is more disconcerting than going somewhere, only to find that there's no easy way out. Also, try to provide an interesting exit. While "out" might function perfectly as an exit, it's boring. Be descriptive. Try "swim" or "fly" or "jump" to describe your exits.
3. You don't have to build everything. While you may be trying to create a castle of your dreams, you don't need to create every intervening step between your grand hall and your bedroom. Be creative; remember, the rules of physics don't necessarily apply here.
4. Use brief descriptions and try to write them beforehand. If you describe a room or an object in flowery prose that stretches for pages, no one will read it. Be brief but descriptive and perfect your description on paper rather than online.
5. Don't describe objects that don't exist! If you mention that there's a neat picture on the wall, create it and give it a good description. People are there to explore and experiment and can get pretty frustrated if they see a description of something they can't touch. On the other hand, you don't need to create everything in your

room to be effective. Describing a rug on the floor is probably better than actually using up your quota creating a thing called a rug that just sits on the floor.

6. Try to build things that fit the theme of the world. It's probably not a good idea to build imaginary strip clubs in the middle of the campus commons of a virtual university just as it would be considered bad form to build a mall smack dab in the middle of a forest on a FurryMUCK.
7. Try to add to the world by building fun and useful objects. Creating things that annoy other people isn't just childish, it's a waste of resources.
8. Clean up after yourself. Creating objects and dropping them all over the place makes an annoying mess because objects can generally be destroyed only by the person who made them, so other players may have trouble removing your trash. Don't throw it away—@recycle it!

Jumping Around

Many virtual worlds let you jump around the world without actually having to cover all the spaces in between. This doesn't mean you should just show up into someone's private space unannounced. Try to use an @page or @mail command to contact someone before you drop by—it's considered just as rude to show up unexpectedly on a virtual community as it is in real life.

There are public spaces, usually described as bars, conference rooms or meeting halls where it is perfectly OK to just pop in. However, you should try to know where you're going before you go there and start babbling away. If someone is giving a lecture, it's bad form to show up and start talking. Online no one's words look any different from anyone else's, so if you start talking in the middle of a lecture or a meeting, your words interfere with someone else's conversation.

Stealing

Unlike most MUDs, stuff that people have usually stays around after they've logged off. This means that a person's house is usually filled with things they've made or collected from the MOO. Unfortunately, if you create something and forget to use the @lock command to make sure that it stays where you put it, anyone can walk off with it. If you come across something that isn't @locked, don't just pick it up and take off with it. Just like in real life, taking things that aren't yours is considered stealing. People can get pretty angry at you if you trundle off with a project they've been working on. If you see something you like, find out who made it and ask the creator how you can make your own. Not only will you end up with a cool object, but you might learn a fair bit about MOO programming.

Tread Lightly

The best way to make sure you don't step on any virtual toes while online is to avoid doing anything that might remotely be considered outrageous until you've been a member of the community for a while. There's really no way to tell how long "a while" is but you'll probably know when the time is right. If you aren't sure about something, politely ask someone for advice before you go charging ahead. If you have a great idea for building something, it'd probably be prudent to ask one of the wizards before you build it. They won't be offended and you'll probably be praised for your consideration. Above all, use your head and try to use some common sense.

Virtual Community

Remembering your manners and acting civilized while online is an important part of being a MUDder. The people who create MUDs and other virtual worlds have spent a lot of time and resources to create a place where you come to be entertained or enlightened. Don't take advantage of their goodwill by being obnoxious or destructive. Remember, too, that if you get out of hand, it's just as easy for the owners of the MUD to delete your character as it was for them to create it.

While online, you are part of an online community of people interacting, building and playing together. You can get more enjoyment out of your experiences online if you try to give something back to the community. I know that this sounds kind of hokey, but it's really true. Contributing your time and resources to building the online communities can not only be rewarding, but fun too.

Getting Involved

Get involved with online councils and discussion groups. Oftentimes, the gods of the world you inhabit are probably dying to have people help out with the day-to-day administration of the world. Try asking if you can help.

Once you've gotten more experienced, one of the greatest services you can perform is being a newbie helper. As you've started your virtual world explorations, you're probably finding out just how confusing and lonely it can be to be the newbie on the block. Wouldn't it be nice to have someone around who could show you the ropes? Some MUDs and other worlds even have a system of high-level players who take turns online as newbie helpers, staying in public places and offering advice, hints and extra equipment to new players. On MOOs and other virtual communities you can do the same thing, offering programming advice and help to new players. After all, these worlds exist, not to make money, but because people believe in working together to provide entertainment and knowledge to others.

Wizardly Ways

Once that great day comes when you've achieved Wizard status on a virtual world, you'll find that with power comes a whole new set of responsibilities. Use your powers wisely to build the world, not to carry on vendettas and petty games. Resist the temptation to abuse your powers—just because you can turn someone into a toad doesn't mean you have to. Probably the greatest responsibility of a wizard is to respect the privacy of others and to leave things alone.

Moving On

Paying attention to etiquette online means using a bit of common sense and some sensitivity to the ways of the worlds. Online etiquette exists to make your life easier, not to stifle your fun.

In the next chapter, we'll surf the cutting edge of virtual world technology by looking at how MUDs and MOOs are being combined with the World Wide Web, and how online worlds may become the virtual conference centers, libraries and universities of tomorrow. It's not every day you get a chance to see the future. Let's go!

7

THE FUTURE

If you've learned one thing during our travels through the online universe, it's that there's something for everyone. After typing a few commands into your computer, you're visiting strange lands and exploring new worlds. Add a few keystrokes, and you're battling monsters, or partying with werewolves in alternate universes on a MUD. Change a few of those commands and you're meeting new friends and working to build a new universe on a MOO. The simple combination of text, computers and the Internet has resulted in almost limitless worlds to discover and explore.

But what's ahead for the world of online realities? Like all other aspects of technology, no one is resting on their laurels when it comes to innovation. As we've seen in our brief excursions into MUD and MOO history, much has changed over the past few years, and the frenzy of development continues to build. Today, we build worlds out of words, but tomorrow you can be sure that text-based worlds will morph into graphical universes where people can meet, play and work online in ways that we can only begin to imagine.

Let's venture forth on the Net to the World Wide Web and look at several attempts to meld the multimedia of the Web with the interactive possibilities of MOOs. After that, we'll drop by LambdaMOO to see one way MOOs might become the virtual libraries of tomorrow. Then we'll check out some of the first virtual conference centers on the Internet and visit what may be the prototype of the university of the future. Finally, we'll get a glimpse at how *Hotwired* magazine is using MOOs to create online meeting places that readers can access from within the magazine.

As you can tell, there's some cool stuff happening.

When Worlds Collide: The World Wide Web Meets the World of MOO

One of the most interesting virtual world innovations has been the combination of MOOs with the World Wide Web. The World Wide Web (the Web) is a global system linking vast amounts of information. Through the combination of a universal system for information transmission and powerful graphic front-end programs called browsers, the Web allows ordinary people to access vast amounts of information quickly and easily, without the steep learning curve that used to slow budding infonauts. However, what's getting people really excited about the Web is that it allows them to view graphics, text, sounds and even video over the Net. By combining the telecommunications capabilities of the Net with the powerful linkage technology of hypertext, the World Wide Web allows us to access the online world with a click of the mouse. You'll remember that MOOs are designed to be object-oriented environments. All the information that makes up a MOO world is stored in a tightly organized database of "objects." Everything, from the most generic blob to the most complex 'bot, is stored in the MOO database in a way that can easily be accessed and examined.

This tightly organized structure makes MOOs ideal for experiments in linking virtual worlds to the World Wide Web. Because MOO information is stored in an easily accessible format, people have been able to develop several new ways to get the Web to read and display MOO information. These systems allow you to log onto a MOO though the Web and then use a simple system of pointing and clicking to perform basic MOO functions. At this time, the Web is not sophisticated enough to handle real-time two-way interaction, so all you can do is act like a ghost in the MOO, flitting from place to place, examining objects and looking at people.

The World Wide Web You can get a great introduction to the World Wide Web by checking out The Mosaic *Quick Tour* books or *Walking the World Wide Web*, all published by Ventana Press. The *Mosaic Quick Tour* is available in both Macintosh and Windows versions. It not only holds your hand as you set up Mosaic for the first time, but also provides some nifty tips about building your own pages and getting around the Web.

The Chiba City Sprawl

Looking back to your earlier visits to The Sprawl, you might remember several references to URLs and the Web in the descriptions of the common areas. In fact, you may have even visited the famous Webster's Bar and URL and wondered what all that gibberish scrawled on the walls was.

That barroom wall gibberish is URLs. On the Web, a site's URL (uniform resource locator) functions as its World Wide Web address, telling your browser how and where to retrieve a certain chunk of information. When you create a "page" on the Web, its URL is its address. Using this address, people can then use their browser to view your page.

So what does all this have to do with The Sprawl? After all, it's just a MOO and doesn't really have anything to do with the World Wide Web, right? In fact, the SprawlMOO is just half the package. Not only can you access The Sprawl through telnet or a client program, but you can access it through the Web at http://chiba.picosof.com:7777. There, you'll find The Sprawl home page, a Web document packed with information about The Sprawl, its creators, a brief bit about how the Web/MOO interface works and a link so that you can log onto the MOO from within the Web. Figure 7-1 shows what you'll see when you arrive at The Sprawl's WWW homepage.

First, connect to The Sprawl's WWW page by pointing your Web browser at http://chiba.picosof.com:7777/. Once you arrive, follow the directions on the screen to go to the page where you can log onto the MOO. If you skipped Chapter 5 and don't have a character on The Sprawl, that's fine—it'll allow you to log on as a guest if you just want to poke around.

Once you log onto The Sprawl through the Web, the WOO (Web+MOO) Transaction Protocol (developed at SenseMedia, the creator of The Sprawl) takes over, transforming your World Wide Web actions into commands that the MOO can understand. The WOO also renders the details of the MOO database into a form that can be used from the World Wide Web. Figure 7-2 shows you what 100 Chiba Blvd., the entrance to The Sprawl, looks like from the WWW.

At first glance, it really doesn't look all that different from what you're used to seeing on The Sprawl. Sure, the text may look prettier, but what you see contains the same information you've seen before—the name of the room, the description of what you see, a list of objects in the room and a list of people

World Wide Web/MOO interface research If you're interested in finding out more about World Wide Web/MOO interface research and technology, subscribe to the moo-www mailing list by sending a message containing the word *subscribe* to moo-www-request@maths.tcd.ie. In addition to examining World Wide Web/MOO interfaces, this list explores research into using MOOs to access the Web, as well as two-way WWW/MOO interfaces.

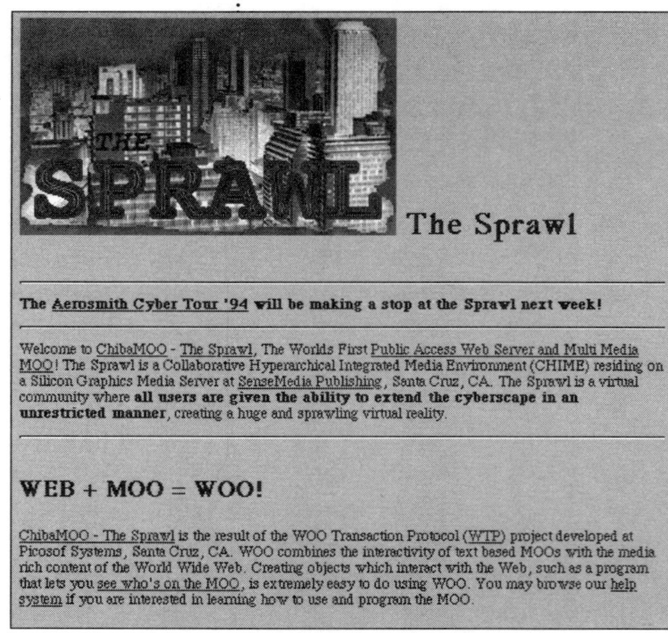

Figure 7-1: *Enter the future at The Sprawl's home page.*

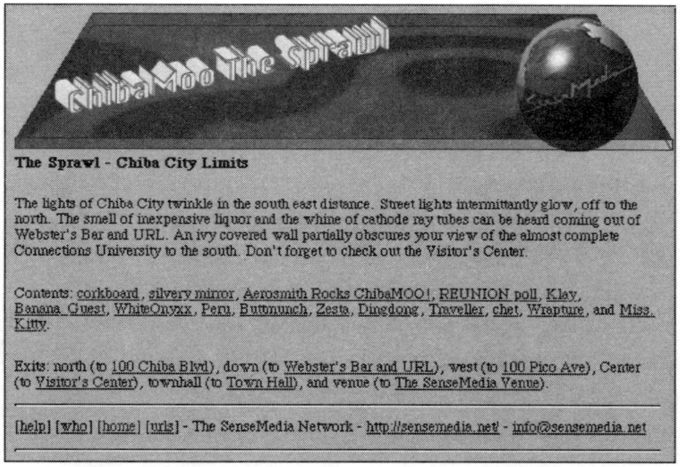

Figure 7-2: *100 Chiba Blvd., as seen though the Web-MOO interface.*

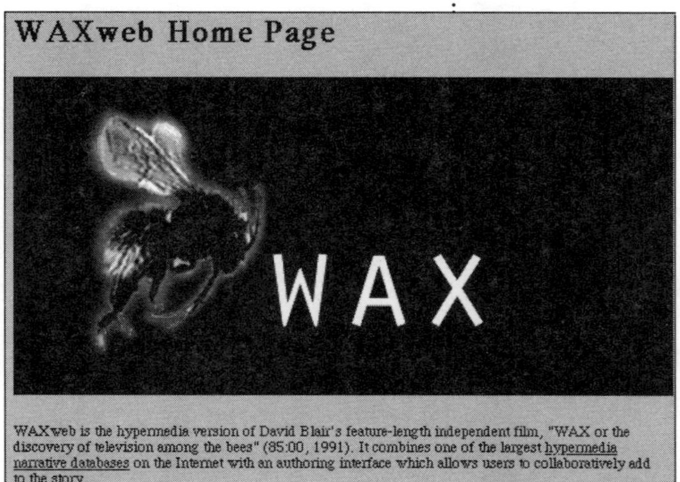

Figure 7-3: *WAXWeb.*

hanging out. Perhaps the most obvious difference (besides the nice text and the big graphic) is that some of what you see is underlined. If you've had any experience walking the Web, you know that an underlined word is a link to another part of the Web. Here, you'll notice that objects—people, exits and things—are underlined. If you click an object, you'll bring up the text associated with it. For example, if you click an exit, you'll go to the place that the exit connects you to. If you click a person or a thing, you'll see a description of that person or thing.

You'll also notice some links along the bottom of the page: [help], [who], [home], [urls]. Clicking these brings up more information—the help button gives you help on using the MOO, the who button tells you who else is online and the home button transports you to your home page. However, the most interesting button is the urls button, because clicking this takes you to Webster's Bar and URL. Here, people have created links to various places on the Web. Since you're already on the Web, you can jump out to the rest of the world just by clicking one of them. You can now access the entire world from within a MOO.

WAXWeb: MOO & Web as Collaborative Art

Even though The Sprawl's marriage of MOO and Web is an interesting experiment, it only scratches the surface of what's possible when a powerful system for distributing multimedia information is paired with an equally powerful way of bringing people together in a virtual space.

WAXWeb is one attempt at using the Web and a MOO to bring people together in a totally new way. This new collaboration exploits the capabilities of each technology to create an art-work that delights and defies description, but also constantly grows and mutates.

WAXWeb, located on the Web at http://bug.village.virginia.edu/, is an ongoing hypermedia project based on filmmaker David Blair's film *WAX, or the Discovery of Television among the Bees. WAX* was the first film to be transmitted across the Internet over the MBone, a high-speed, high-capacity link that allows real-time transmission of sound and video.

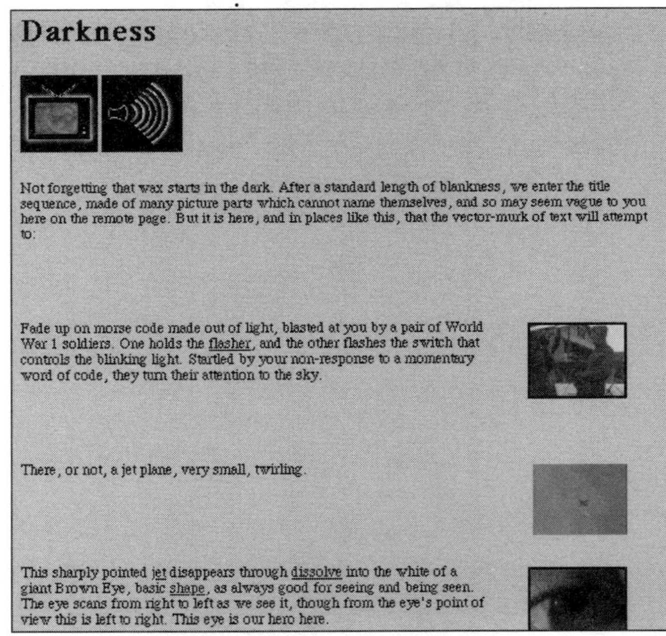

Figure 7-4: *"Darkness," the first hypernode in the WAXWeb.*

When you visit WAXWeb you have access to more than 1,500 stills from the movie, 500 video clips and 2,000 audio clips, all linked together though the World Wide Web in a series of "hypernodes." Figure 7-4 shows you "Darkness," the first hypernode on WAXWeb.

What's really innovative about WAXWeb is that it allows you to access its companion WaxMOO. WaxMOO allows you to interact with other people visiting WAXWeb and to use the programming capabilities of the MOO to add your own multimedia information to WAXWeb. Through this combination of the hypermedia capabilities of the Web and the interactive qualities of MOOs, WAXWeb has become a dynamic work of art, constantly changing and always growing. Because the WaxMOO allows people interested in the project to meet online, WAXWeb is perhaps the first work of art that maintains an interactive online art forum.

Cardiff WWW/MOO Server

After WAXWeb, you might be surprised at just how ordinary Cardiff University's WWW/MOO server home page looks. Don't let the simplicity fool you—there's a lot of stuff going on here. Located at http://www.cm.cf.ac.uk/User/Andrew.Wilson/CardiffMOO, the CardiffMOO home page serves as the nexus for MOO-net, a worldwide network of MOOs that are experimenting with World Wide Web interfaces. From here, you can jump off to Web rooms at LambdaMOO, the MediaMOO, Diversity University and BlueMOOn. Also, without leaving the World Wide Web, you can take a peek at who's online at any of 10 different MOOs from around the world.

Figure 7-5: *The CardiffMOO home page.*

This experiment is still in its beginning stages, something that you'll discover if you have as many problems getting its links to work as I did. However, you can get a good look at the future of WWW/MOO interfaces by going to Between Worlds—CardiffMOO's home room on the Web.

Figure 7-6 shows you what you'll find when you arrive at Between Worlds. On the surface, it resembles what we saw when we entered The Sprawl through the Web. There's all the basic stuff—room name, description and lists of objects—but you'll also notice that the movement links have been moved to their own section near the bottom and that some links have been embedded in the description.

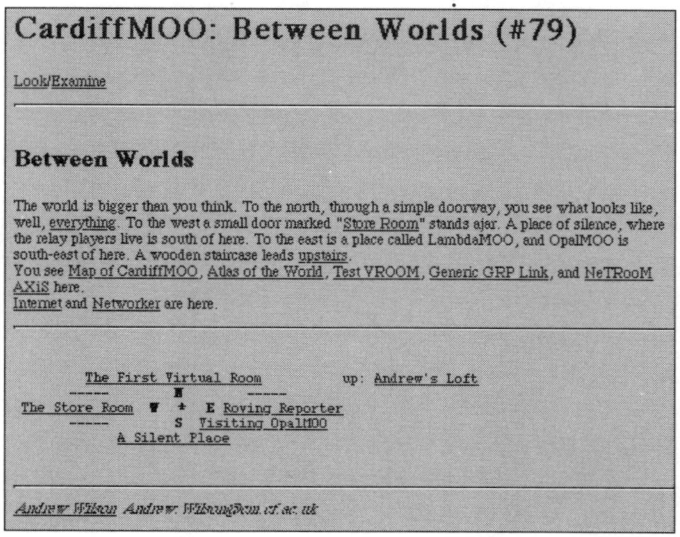

Figure 7-6: *Between Worlds at CardiffMOO.*

These links near the description are where things begin to really get interesting. Unlike The Sprawl's links, most of these aren't just links to other descriptions. Instead, CardiffMOO utilizes a unique system that embeds graphic information within the MOO. Clicking the "Map of CardiffMOO" brings up an actual graphic map of the MOO (Figure 7-7), which shows us where we are and where we can go. Unfortunately, you can't go to any of the places on the map by clicking them—you have to use the movement system for that. Even so, this ability to use graphics for objects represents a big step for MOO/WWW combinations. Up this point, MOOs couldn't use anything except text to describe objects within the MOO. Now they can.

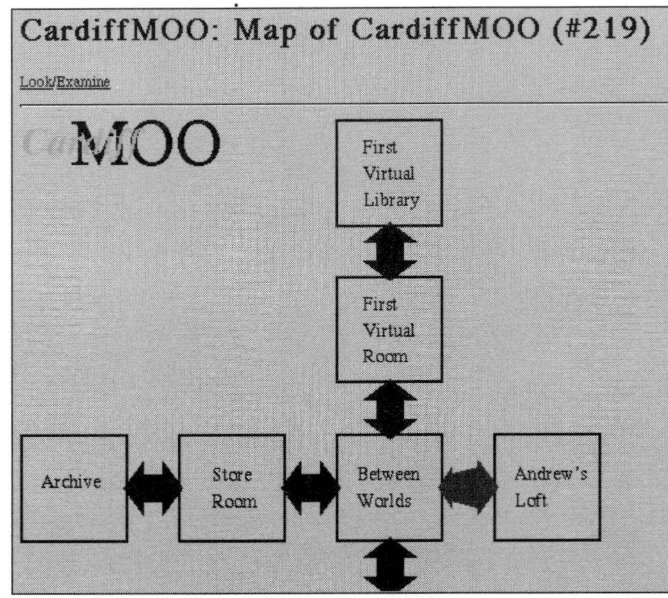

Figure 7-7: *The CardiffMOO Map.*

Hypertext Hotel: A Hypertext Work-in-Progress

We'll end our tour through the world of World Wide Web/MOO experiments by stopping off at Hypertext Hotel. You can get there by pointing your WWW browser at: **http://duke.cs.brown.edu:8888/**.

The Hypertext Hotel is a great example of how you don't need to use graphics to create an interesting document on the Web, especially if you throw a MOO into the mix. Hypertext Hotel is the current version of a work of hypertext fiction begun by hyper-guru Robert Coover during his hypertext fiction seminar at Brown University.

First of all, you might be wondering what hypertext fiction is. We've already seen that hypertext (and hypermedia) is a system for linking information in a way that allows a reader to follow links to other information. It's easy to see how this could be useful for associating a bunch of facts or following references in a paper, but how can hypertext be used for writing fiction? Isn't fiction supposed to be read from beginning to end? After all, everyone knows how peeking at the end of a mystery novel ruins the whole story (even though we all do it anyway!). How can a book that allows us to jump around within it work? Actually, the anxiety you feel when confronted with a hypertext book is exactly the kind of feeling that people writing hypertext fiction want you to feel. Hypertext fiction is designed to shake up all your current perceptions about what a book should be and make you look at fiction in a new way.

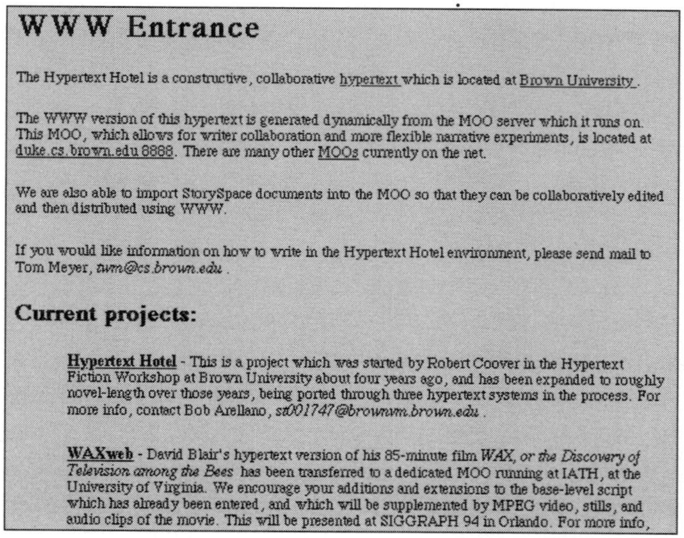

WWW Entrance

The Hypertext Hotel is a constructive, collaborative hypertext which is located at Brown University.

The WWW version of this hypertext is generated dynamically from the MOO server which it runs on. This MOO, which allows for writer collaboration and more flexible narrative experiments, is located at duke.cs.brown.edu 8888. There are many other MOOs currently on the net.

We are also able to import StorySpace documents into the MOO so that they can be collaboratively edited and then distributed using WWW.

If you would like information on how to write in the Hypertext Hotel environment, please send mail to Tom Meyer, *twm@cs.brown.edu*.

Current projects:

Hypertext Hotel - This is a project which was started by Robert Coover in the Hypertext Fiction Workshop at Brown University about four years ago, and has been expanded to roughly novel-length over those years, being ported through three hypertext systems in the process. For more info, contact Bob Arellano, *st001747@brownvm.brown.edu*.

WAXweb - David Blair's hypertext version of his 85-minute film *WAX, or the Discovery of Television among the Bees* has been transferred to a dedicated MOO running at IATH, at the University of Virginia. We encourage your additions and extensions to the base-level script which has already been entered, and which will be supplemented by MPEG video, stills, and audio clips of the movie. This will be presented at SIGGRAPH 94 in Orlando. For more info,

Figure 7-8: *The Hypertext Hotel home page.*

While all this may sound pretty heavy, the experience of jumping into the Hypertext Hotel is as fun as it is unsettling. Each page is usually a brief but lyrical description of a scene at this imaginary hotel, and you never know where the links from that page are going to take you. Whether you find the experience enlightening or disturbing probably rests as much on what links you take as it does the text you read.

Other works of hypertext fiction exist on the Web, but what makes the Hypertext Hotel so interesting (and relevant to our discussion of online worlds) is that what you see on the Web is being generated from the HypertextHotel MOO. Just as we've seen before, the Web pages are generated from the HypertextHotel MOO database. Because Hypertext Hotel is combined with a MOO, you can log on and create your own links and text in the story. Because you're on a MOO, you can participate in online discussions about Hypertext Hotel and hypertext in general. Just like WAXWeb, Hypertext Hotel combines WWW's linking capability with the immediacy and collaboration of MOOs to create an ever-changing document and a forest of forking paths.

Looking It Up Online

Not only are people using the World Wide Web to access MOO information, but now people are using MOOs to access information from within MOOs themselves. The Internet Gopher is a system of linked information servers that use menus to provide access to tens of thousands of pages of information on just about anything you can imagine. Because Gophers search and access information over the Internet, and because Gopher systems are almost entirely text based, they're an ideal partner for exploring information retrieval from within a MOO.

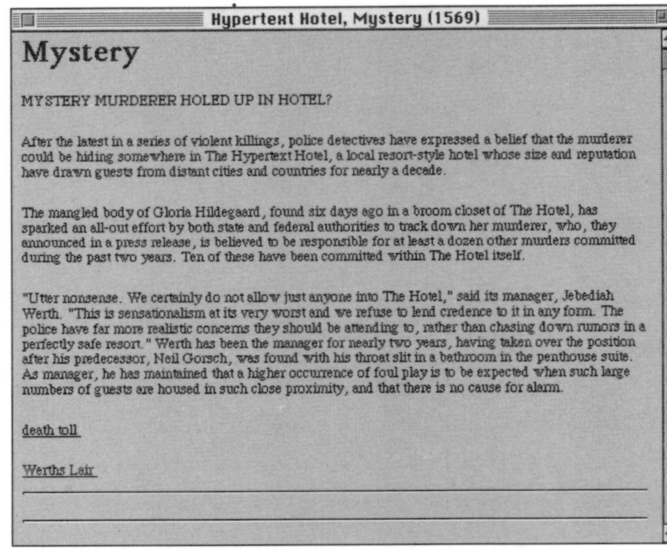

Figure 7-9: *A page from Hypertext Hotel.*

Virtual Libraries

Larry Masinter of the Xerox Palo Alto Research Center and Erik Ostrom of Gustavus Adolphus College are information researchers who are using MOO technology to develop libraries of the future. In their paper "Collaborative Information Retrieval: Gopher From a MOO" they foresee a future where the Internet provides a place for research and discussion. MOOs provide a perfect place for this, because they already contain programming features that allow easy linkage to information servers (Gophers) as well as facilities where people can interact. By bringing people together in a MOO and allowing them to access information, Masinter and Ostrom give us a look at what research might be like in the future.

Gopher in a MOO

Masinter and Ostrom have built a virtual library on Jays House MOO, a popular MOO located at jayshouse.ccs.neu.edu 1709. Once you arrive at Jays House, you can follow a simple set of commands to bring you to the Library, a room within the MOO where you can use a "Gopher Slate" to look up information.

The Gopher Slate is like a small, powerful computer that allows you to look up information quickly and easily. Using commands such as look and pick, you can examine the Gopher menus and move through them, accessing information by "picking" it from a menu. Once you access information, it appears onscreen just like anything else you might see on the MOO—you can even use special commands to collect the information and mail it to yourself for later reading. It's even possible for several people to look up information at once—a welcome feature for people doing group research. The whole experience is a lot like meeting your friends at the school library and doing research together, but with the added ease of having massive amounts of information at your fingertips at all times.

Perhaps, using technologies like the Gopher Slate, the virtual libraries of the future won't be sterile "information retrieval centers" but places to read and talk with other people from all over the world. In fact, it's not hard to imagine a day where "meet me at the library" means "meet me on the MOO!"

Online Learning

If brainstorming with your friends at a virtual library without leaving your house sounds exciting, then you'll probably do backflips when you hear that someday it'll be possible to go to school, meet with friends and colleagues to discuss your current research, and attend conferences online. Just imagine—no more dragging yourself to the shower for that dreaded 8 a.m. class, no more frantic travel to conferences, and no more worries about what you're going to wear to school. Instead, you can show up as you are by turning on your computer, typing a few commands and logging onto your favorite virtual schools, meeting places and online conference centers. MOO technology makes it all possible.

Diversity University

Someday, all schools might look like Diversity University. Even though it's still in its early stages of construction, DU already sports a well-stocked library, a spacious student center, many classrooms and an inviting commons where you can hang out and chat with fellow students. Better yet, there's no tuition and no one cares if you show up to class in your underwear—Diversity University is located entirely on a MOO.

Diversity University is associated with the Globewide Network Academy, an organization dedicated to developing a fully accredited online university. Here, you can attend classes and lectures with people from all over the world on subjects from modern literature to biology. Classes are held in virtual "classrooms" where students and teachers meet online. Also, Diversity University has a well-stocked online library where you can go to read any of the hundreds of reference works stored on DU or use its MOO-Gopher interface to look up information from any of thousands of Gopher servers from around the world. When you want to take a break, head to the commons or visit the student center, where you'll be sure to meet fellow coeds.

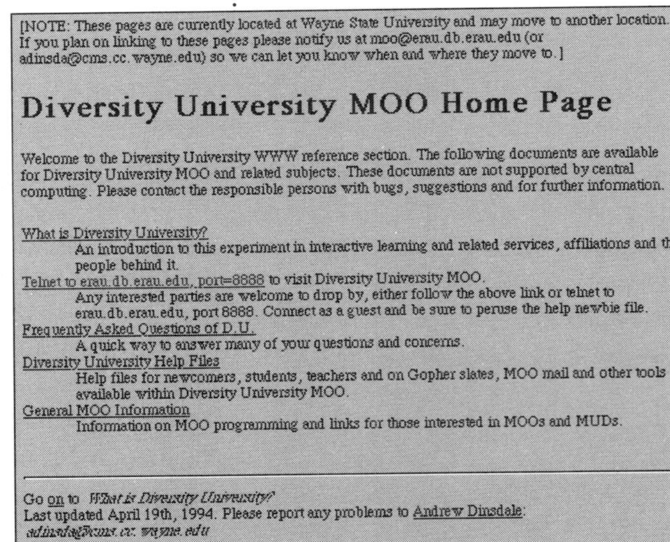
[NOTE: These pages are currently located at Wayne State University and may move to another location. If you plan on linking to these pages please notify us at moo@erau.db.erau.edu (or adinsda@cms.cc.wayne.edu) so we can let you know when and where they move to.]

Diversity University MOO Home Page

Welcome to the Diversity University WWW reference section. The following documents are available for Diversity University MOO and related subjects. These documents are not supported by central computing. Please contact the responsible persons with bugs, suggestions and for further information.

What is Diversity University?
An introduction to this experiment in interactive learning and related services, affiliations and the people behind it.
Telnet to erau.db.erau.edu, port=8888 to visit Diversity University MOO.
Any interested parties are welcome to drop by, either follow the above link or telnet to erau.db.erau.edu, port 8888. Connect as a guest and be sure to peruse the help newbie file.
Frequently Asked Questions of D.U.
A quick way to answer many of your questions and concerns.
Diversity University Help Files
Help files for newcomers, students, teachers and on Gopher slates, MOO mail and other tools available within Diversity University MOO.
General MOO Information
Information on MOO programming and links for those interested in MOOs and MUDs.

Go on to *What is Diversity University?*
Last updated April 19th, 1994. Please report any problems to Andrew Dinsdale:
adinsda@cms.cc.wayne.edu

Figure 7-10: *Diversity University's WWW home page.*

Diversity University was created by Jeanne Butler McWhorter, a graduate student at the University of Houston. She originally intended DU as a place where she could meet other social workers to share ideas and research. However, as word about her online meeting place spread across the Net, more people began to visit Diversity University and it grew into something much more than an online social worker clubhouse. If you want to be a part of this ongoing experiment in online learning, telnet to moo.du.org 8888 or check out the Diversity University home page on the World Wide Web, located at http://pass.wayne.edu/DU.html. Figure 7-10 shows what you'll find when you get there.

Virtual Conference Centers

Judging by the number of professional conferences held every year, it's clear that people with similar professional interests love getting together. However, time and university budgets usually put a limit on how often people from different parts of the world can have meetings. For years, researchers have relied on the Internet and the telephone as a way of staying in touch between meetings, but e-mail and conference calls can't take the place of conferences. Even though a conference call allows you to talk to several people at once, you can't share a whole paper with other people over the phone. Conversely, e-mail is a good way to transmit papers and other research materials, but it lacks the spontaneity of actually being able to discuss things as a group.

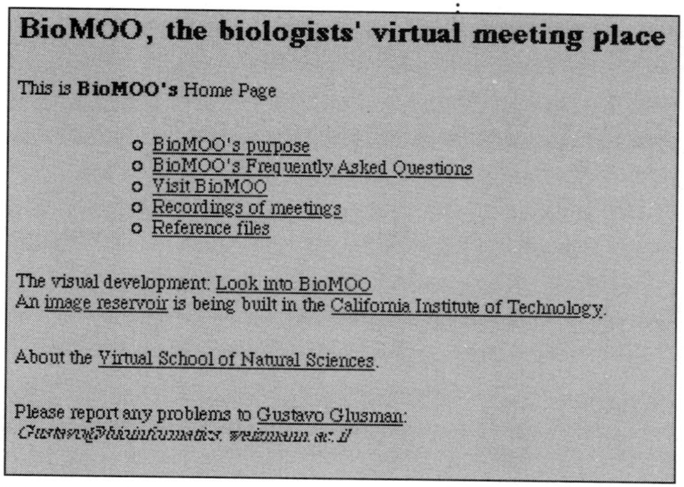

Figure 7-11: *The BioMOO home page.*

MOOs change all that. Now, people can get together and share information no matter where they are, and they can do it in the same spontaneous, interactive way that they do when they are physically in the same place. Using a MOO, you can hold a virtual "lecture" where everyone gets the chance to listen in and see the entire text of the lecture scroll up their screens. After seeing the lecture, virtual conference-goers can use the chatting capabilities of a MOO to discuss the paper, regardless of where they are. Because of the capabilities that MOOs offer for online research discussions, it should come as no surprise that there are several "virtual conference centers" on the Net already.

BioMOO

BioMOO bills itself as "the biologists' virtual meeting place," a pretty apt description of this online meeting space for biologists. Located at the Weizmann Institute of Science in Israel (telnet to bioinformatics.weizman.ac.il 8888, if you want to check it out), BioMOO is an online community of biological researchers and a space for virtual conferences, meetings and roundtable discussions. Additionally, BioMOO has its own World Wide Web space where people can present *conference posters*. These documents utilize the technology of the Web to include graphics from current research, links to other research and even sound and video. If you want to see some of the posters that are being presented on BioMOO, go to http://bioinformatics.weizmann.ac.il:70/1s/biomoo. Figure 7-11 shows the BioMOO home page. Figure 7-12 gives an example of an online research poster.

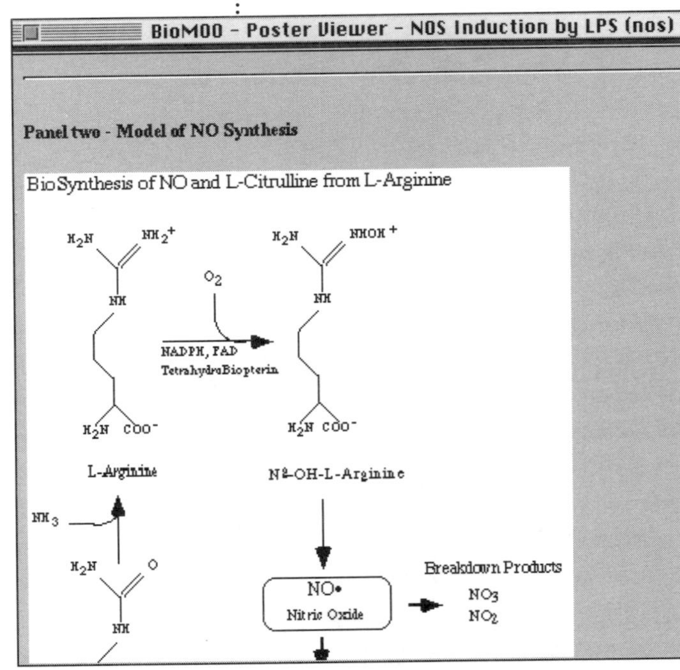

Figure 7-12: *A poster presented on the BioMOO WWW site.*

BioMOO gives us a glimpse at the future of professional communication. Now, rather than hopping on a plane to learn about current research at a conference, you can use the Web to see what people are up to. And, because World Wide Web pages can be updated in a matter of seconds, you can be sure that the research you see is the very latest. After you've used the Web to take a tour around the virtual conference center, you can jump over to the MOO to discuss the work you've seen or meet with colleagues. If you're involved in biological research, you'll probably be able to buy a few more petri dishes with the money you save by meeting your peers on BioMOO.

PMC MOO

Scientists and computer researchers aren't the only ones using MOOs as virtual conference centers—people in the humanities are starting to see the potential of online, interactive communication. Probably the most well known humanities MOO is PMC-MOO, an online community created and run by the people of the *Postmodern Culture* electronic journal. PMC MOO is a virtual community of writers, students and theorists using the MOO as a virtual conference center and meeting place. There, they share current research papers, hold virtual symposia and gather informally to discuss postmodern culture and the changing role of communication in the information age. In fact, PMC MOO is a natural extension of the *PMC Journal*, one of the first peer-reviewed electronic journals available over the Internet. You can visit the PMC-MOO home page and journal archives on the World Wide Web at: http://jefferson.village.virginia.edu/pmc/pmc-moo.html.

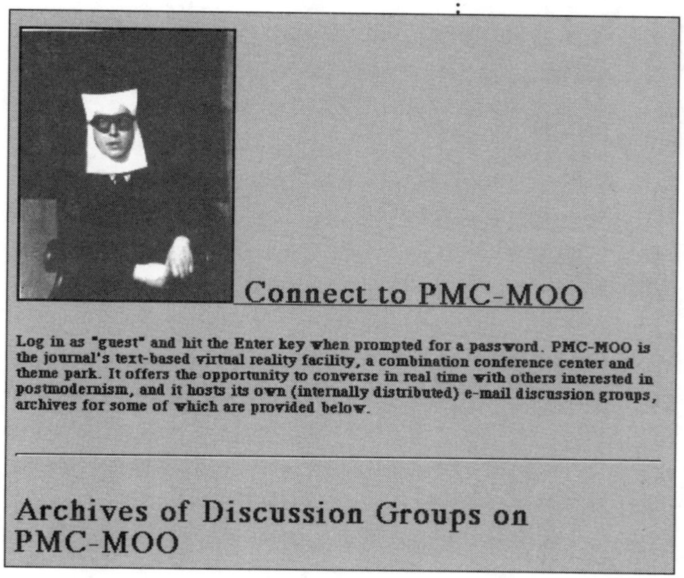

Figure 7-13: *The PMC-MOO home page gives you a hint what's in store on the PMC-MOO.*

The PMC-MOO uses its facilities not only as a place to meet, but as a private forum where people can discuss their research away from the everyday bustle of their real lives. PMC-MOO has several MOO-only mailing lists and discussion groups for swapping papers. It often holds online lectures and symposia. If you want to drop by to visit, just telnet to pmcdemo@hero.village.virginia.edu. Log on as **guest** and press Enter (or Return) when prompted for a password. From there, follow the instructions to log on as a guest and examine the rest of the MOO. Even if you don't consider yourself on the cutting edge of literary and cultural theory, you're sure to find some interesting people and information on the PMC-MOO.

Using MOOs to Teach Writing: ZooMOO

Finally, one of the most interesting ways that MOOs are being used takes advantage of the nature of MOOs themselves. Since MOOs are text-based virtual realities, they provide a great place for people to see how their writing affects other people, because they can create actual worlds that people can enter and interact with. Often, new writing students feel as if their work has no "meaning" for anyone except themselves and their teachers. MOOs gives students the opportunity to see how their words make a difference.

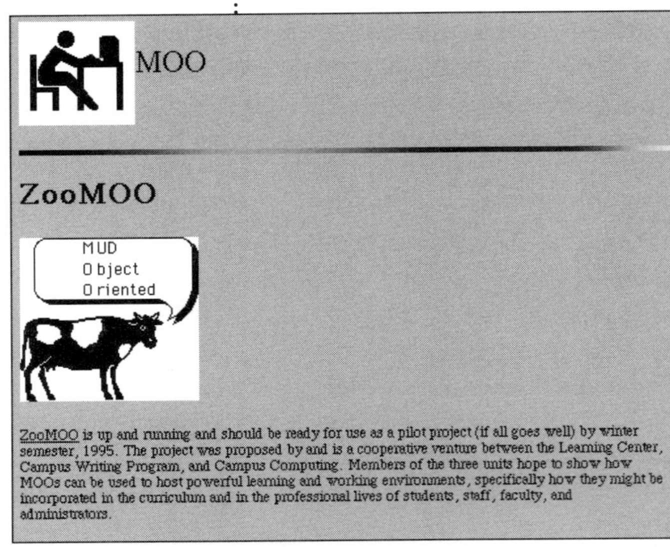

Figure 7-14: *The ZooMOO home page.*

ZooMOO is a virtual world located at the University of Missouri and is the brainchild of Joe Heck, Eric Crump (who, incidentally, edits a section of the Hypertext Hotel called RhetNet) and Sally Foster, all faculty members at MU. Designed as a cooperative project by the Learning Center, the Campus Writing Program and the Campus Computing department at MU, ZooMOO looks like it's going to be the first project of its kind to take students online and use the capabilities of the MOO to help them become better writers. In addition, ZooMOO sees itself as a place where students, faculty, administration and staff can meet and share their professional experiences. ZooMOO isn't up and running yet, but you can get more information about it from the Zoo MOO home page, located at http://www.missouri.edu/~wleric/moo.html.

Graphical Interfaces

Virtual communities have been text-based so far, but the limited experiments that have combined the World Wide Web with the world of MOOs have shown us a glimpse of what can happen when we combine graphics with MOOs. However, not all MOO graphics are on the Web—today people are looking at new ways to change text-based online virtual realities into graphical worlds. At this point in the development of the online world, the results are a long way from the hype we so often see on TV about "virtual reality," but if we're going to look into the future of online worlds, it's important to look at some of the first steps people are taking to make graphic MUDs.

BSX-Graphical MUDding

Graphical MUDs have been around for a few years, but only with the availability of relatively cheap high-speed modems have they begun to grow in popularity. The grandfather of all graphical MUDs is BSX MUD at Lysator University.

Figure 7-15 shows a scene from BSX MUD. It might not give many Nintendo games a run for their money, but it does show how a little ingenuity can go a long way. To access a BSX MUD you use a special client, which you can download from ftp.lysator.liu.se in the pub/lpmud/bsx directory. Once you download the BSX client (available for X-Windows, Amiga, Macintosh and MS-DOS machines), you use it to connect to bsxmud.lysator.liu.se 7475. Once you've logged on, your BSX client transforms special formatting codes transmitted by BSX MUD into pictures like the one you see in Figure 7-15.

Figure 7-15: *A typical BSX MUD scene.*

You move around in BSX MUD by using the familiar LPMud commands. Moving, searching and talking to other characters are handled the same way that you're used to, but objects, people and places that you normally would just read about are rendered into images by the client program. Using a BSX MUD is a little like using a keyboard to control an illustrated storybook, turning the pages with commands rather than your fingers. Soon, you stop paying attention to the simplicity of the graphics. It's easy to get sucked into long sessions on BSX as you wait to see what's around the next turn.

Even though the graphics of BSX aren't going to win any special-effects awards, the system presents some interesting possibilities for the MUDs of the future. As modem speeds increase and the prices of sophisticated graphical computer systems decrease, we're sure to see more MUDs with pictures. In fact, several commercial services have begun to use similar (though more graphically sophisticated) methods to create "gaming networks" where people can play games against each other online. Networked, multi-player games are becoming a hot commodity with computer entertainment people, because they're starting to realize that computers just can't replace people as sophisticated opponents. Of course, as a member of the online universe, you already know this—everyone else is just now catching up to you.

Into the Future

If our explorations of the online universe and the future of virtual worlds have taught us anything, it's that giving people the tools to shape their own reality can yield some interesting results. MOOs, MUDs and other online worlds offer the potential to bring people together to do things that have never been possible. In the past, people have often looked at new technology as a "dehumanizing" force that separated people, but perhaps the popularity of virtual worlds and online communities rests on the fact that they bring people together.

What does the future hold? As more people come online, there's as much of a need for increased access to people as there is for increased access to information. The exponential growth in personal communication services (cellular phones and pagers) shows us that. As our lives become more hectic and we spend more time interacting with fax machines, talking car doors and voice mail systems from hell, we'll look for more opportunities to talk to real people. It's uncertain what form these new means of interaction will take, but we can look at *Wired Magazine's* online publication, *Hotwired*, for a clue.

Hotwired arrived on the World Wide Web in November of 1994 as an attempt to make us reexamine how we look at magazines. Not only is *Hotwired* an entirely new publication, separate from its "physical" magazine counterpart, but it provides ways of interacting that aren't possible with "physical" texts. When you read *Hotwired* on the Web, you can follow links to information sources outside the magazine, as well as links to information within the publication itself. Besides having the opportunity to interact with *Hotwired* through the links, you can become part of the editorial staff by suggesting your own links to and from articles. And because it's interactive, *Hotwired* is different every time you visit.

Figure 7-16: Hotwired*'s home page.*

How does this apply to online communities? *Hotwired*'s creators realized that its readers were already a kind of "community" with shared interests in technology, culture and the Internet. The question was how to provide a space where this community of readers could meet. MOOs offered an answer.

Hotwired provides links to a meeting place called Cafe Wired on both LambdaMOO and BayMOO. By clicking one of two links from within the magazine, readers find themselves instantly transported to a virtual cafe populated with other readers. Cafe Wired is more than a virtual hangout, though—it's a place where authors can hold lectures about their work or have virtual book signings where they can chat with readers. In effect, *Hotwired* has created an entirely new medium, one that combines the depth of a magazine with the immediate interactivity of a virtual community. Whether this new medium will take off as a new paradigm for publications and online communication isn't certain, but what is certain is that *Hotwired* gives us a glimpse of the future.

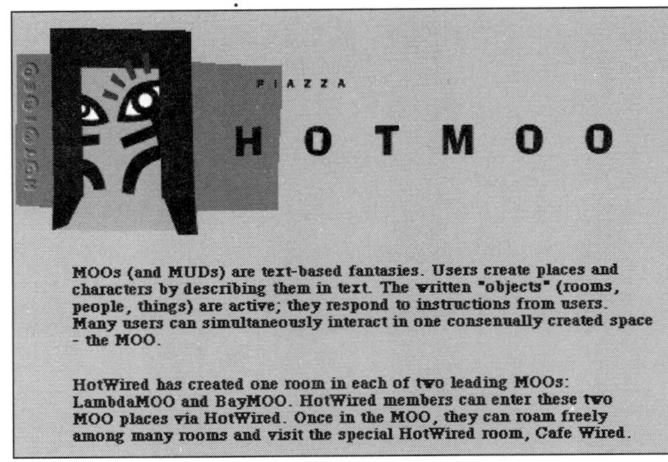

Figure 7-17: Hotwired's *HotMOO page.*

Moving On

The future of life online is bound to be exciting. Virtual worlds are being used to bring people together in ways that have never before been possible, expanding how we interact and promising nearly limitless new directions. We've touched upon some new and innovative ways to use the technology of online worlds. Now it's time to head out on your own virtual world adventures. Chapter 8 is an online atlas and travel guide with directions to some of the best MUDs, MOOs and MUCKs. Happy trails!

8

Online Atlas & Travel Guide

Now that you've had a chance to see a small corner of the online world, you're ready to head out on your own adventures. But the Net's a big place—how are you going to find your way around? Look no further! In this online atlas and travel guide, you'll find a whole mess of MUDs to visit, MOOs to hang out in and even a MUCK or two to poke around in. Cyberspace is a big place, but this guide will make sure you hit all the right spots.

There are hundreds of virtual worlds on the Internet, and it's easy for a newbie to get overwhelmed by the choices. Where do you start? I've gleaned some of the most interesting worlds I've come across and arranged them into a few categories to help you to find one to explore. However, there's a lot of crossover, so take my categorizations with a grain of salt. My best advice is this: if it sounds interesting, check it out! You may be pleasantly surprised.

Ready? Let's log on and see what's out there.

Fantasy

These are lands where magic rules and monsters roam freely. Generally, fantasy worlds let you live out a part in a land of myth and legend.

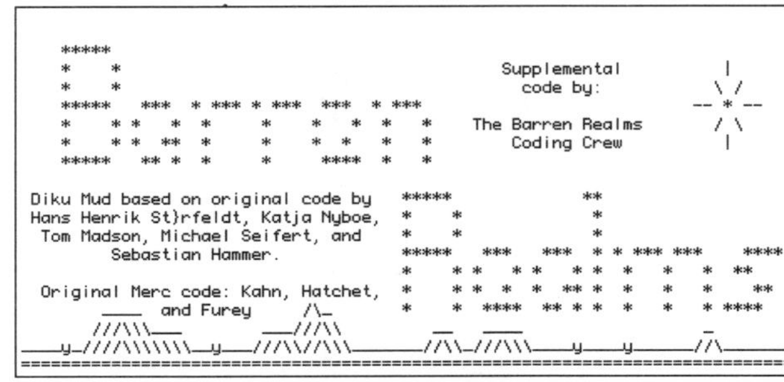

Figure 8-1: *Barren Realms login screen.*

Barren Realms

Addresses:

liii.com 8000

198.207.193.1 8000

Classification: MERCmud

For more info: e-mail barren@liii.com

To enter Barren Realms is to enter a raucous, freewheeling land populated with fantastic creatures and bizarre places. The air of Barren Realms reverberates with the feeling that just about anything can happen, and it usually does. New characters can choose to be any one of five different races, so you can be sure that your interactions with others will be anything but mundane. You'll never get bored adventuring on Barren Realms.

Infinity

Addresses:

sirius.nmt.edu 6715

129.138.4.119 6715

Classification: AberMUD

Infinity is a fantasy world based at New Mexico Tech. If you're looking for a place to hang your virtual hat, do a bit of adventuring and have some fun, this is the place to go. It's not heavily populated, but the people there are friendly and helpful to newbies, so its a good place to go if you're starting out. Though Infinity has its share of magical beings and fantastic locations, it's really a peaceful, easygoing place at heart. Stop by and see for yourself.

Final Realms

Addresses:

kark.hiof.no 2001

158.36.33.5 2001

Classification: LPMud

FAQ available from:

ftp://fr-faq-0.2/pub/FR-MUDFR-faq-0.2

This is the real deal. Final Realms is a very active, incredibly detailed world where role playing and commitment to the MUD are paramount. You can expect no quarter from the other players, so it's a good idea to join one of the guilds and have some friends to watch your back. Once you have survived long enough to rise through the ranks, you can even apply to be a creator (provided you know some LPC programming) and add your own fantastic places to this magical MUD. If role playing, magic and fantasy are your forte, Final Realms may become your final stop in your quest for the perfect MUD.

NANVAENT 3

Addresses:

corrour.cc.strath.ac.uk 3000

130.159.220.8 3000

Classification: LPMud

WWW: http://aragorn.uio.no/nanvaent/

Figure 8-2: *The Nanvaent logo.*

You can only log onto Nanvaent between 5 p.m. and 9 a.m. GMT (that's 12 noon to 4 a.m. EST), but it's worth the wait to get a peek at this fun place. Nanvaent is based on a fantastic world of adventure where just about anybody can find a quest to keep their interest. Here, you can be anything from a human to a wolf, so you can be sure that your visit here will be a step away from your everyday life. There's a great help system and lots of assistance for newbies, so don't be afraid to stop by and check things out.

Sleepless Nights

Addresses:

cs3.brookes.ac.uk 6789

161.73.1.2 6789

Classification: AberMUD

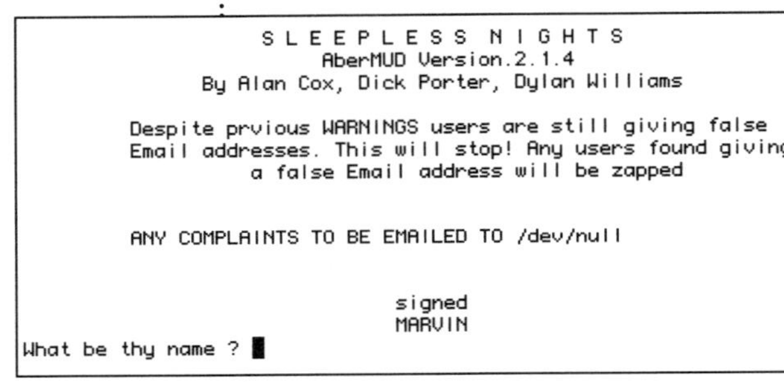

Figure 8-3: *The Sleepless Nights greeting.*

Sleepless Nights is based on a fantasy world that, on the surface, will appear pretty familiar to anyone who's poked around the worlds of MUD for a while. However, what sets Sleepless Nights apart from so many other places is the quality and depth of description in this virtual world. The creators of Sleepless Nights seem to know that good writing is the basis for a good MUD. If you're interested in visiting a world that stays with you after you've left, Sleepless Nights is the place to go.

High Adventure

While many of these worlds have a lot in common with the Fantasy category, the High Adventure places are deadlier and put a higher value on killing monsters, solving quests and exploring new worlds.

BatMUD

Addresses:

bat.cs.hut.fi 23

130.233.40.180 23

Classification: LPMud

WWW: http://bat.cs.hut.fi:81/

Adventuring on BatMUD is like entering a whole new world, and a huge one at that. BatMUD's strengths are in the details: lots and lots of races to choose from, thousands of places to visit, many levels for your character to aspire to, and even a nifty "wish system" to improve yourself. While it may be a tough place to start out, BatMUD is pretty hospitable for newbies, too, because of its great help system and special newbie goodies. The creators of BatMUD have spent a huge amount of time tweaking the MUD until it runs like a complex but efficient machine. Don't let their efforts go to waste—stop by and see just how good MUDding can be.

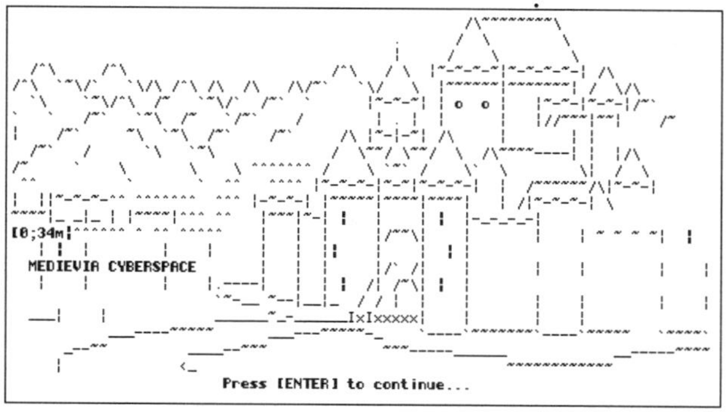

Figure 8-4: *MEDIEVIA Cyberspace's zippy title screen.*

MEDIEVIA Cyberspace

Addresses:

intense.netaxs.com 4000

198.69.186.36 4000

Classification: DikuMUD

MEDIEVIA Cyberspace's theme fits your typical adventure/fantasy categories. However, what set this place apart and make it perfect for new characters are all the extras that the programmers have added. For users with color ANSI terminals, MEDIEVIA has a great color interface that makes play easier and a lot more fun. MEDIEVIA's detailed and well-indexed help system will never leave you scratching your head wondering what verb to use when you're in that difficult situation. MEDIEVIA seems to love having new players, and you'll find several nifty features to help you along as you move from newbie MUDder to wizard (someday). If you're just getting your bearings in Cyberspace, MEDIEVIA should be one of your first stops.

Mortal Combat

Kill or be killed. Worlds in this category all allow player killing and often make it the centerpiece of your time online. They're usually not too cordial to newbies (except as a snack), so be warned!

Empire

Addresses:

einstein.physics.drexel.edu 4000
129.25.1.120 4000

Classification: DikuMUD

For more info: email mud@einstein.physics.drexel.edu

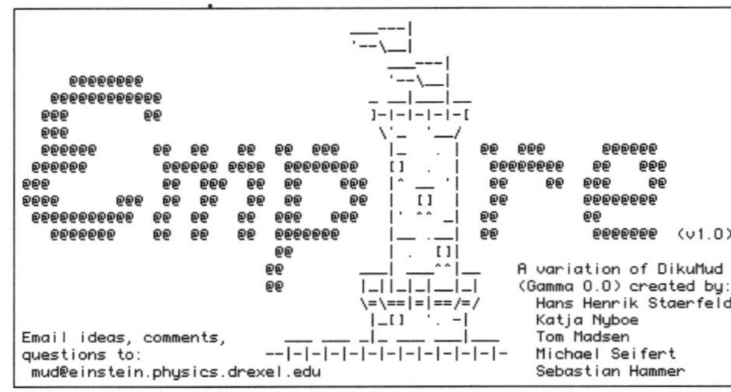

Figure 8-5: *Death awaits on Empire.*

When you step into Empire, you're entering a complex and dangerous world. From the beginning when you create your character, you'll get a hint at the depth of the MUD. You can choose from many different classes and races in your quest to create the perfect character and then tweak your statistics to create the ultimate MUD machine. Choose carefully, though, because once you step into Empire you have to watch your back at every turn—Empire places no restrictions on player killing. Unlike most worlds, which at least give you a safe haven or two to catch your breath, you can be killed anywhere on Empire. The faint-hearted might want to avoid this place, but if you're into a fast and furious game, Empire is probably for you.

Genocide

Addresses:

pip.shsu.edu 2222
192.92.115.10 2222

Classification: LPMud

While some might disagree that Genocide is a MUD, it's sure a lot of fun! Here, there are no quests, no real protracted adventure and pre-

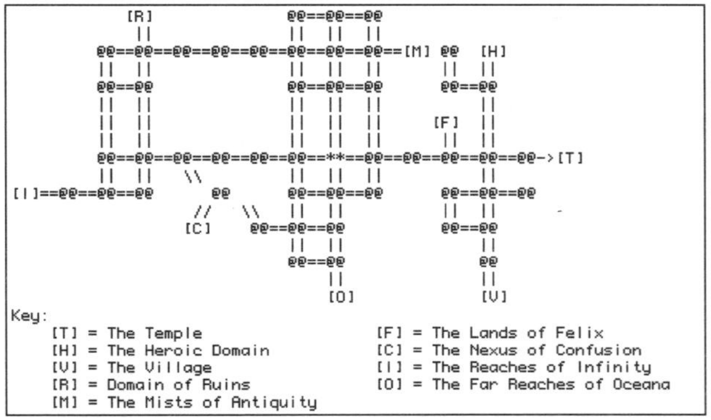

Figure 8-6: *One of the maps available on Genocide.*

cious little chit chat. What you'll find instead is a world where endless wars rage between characters who fight for points and status. When you arrive you're a ghost, a disembodied wisp of a character whose immaterial nature makes it impossible for you to do more than look around and see what you're getting into. But when a war starts, watch out! You materialize into mortal form and scramble about in a wild quest for weapons and territory. Once you've gotten a toehold, it's time to rock as you battle it out with other players. It's fast, it's furious, and there's no other MUD like it.

ZombieMUD

Addresses:

linux1.sjoki.uta.fi 3333

192.98.84.5 3333

Classification: LPMud

ZombieMUD is a place with a big, bad attitude! Fighting for your life is the theme-of-the-day here, where 16 guilds and many different races keep the mix heated to a furious boil. Add in some particularly nasty monsters and some MUD admins with no mercy and you've got a place that'll keep you on your toes every time you visit. If you like your MUDding on the bleeding edge, ZombieMUD might be worth a visit. One caveat, though—because ZombieMUD's such an exciting place to visit, there are a lot of people trying to get on. You may experience some lag, but look on the bright side—it'll give you more time to contemplate your impending doom.

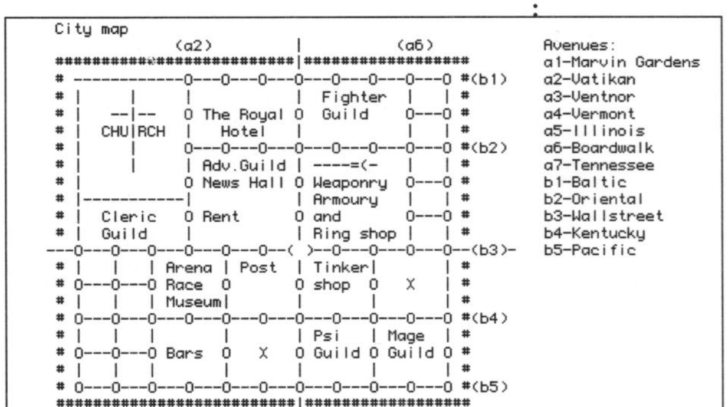

Figure 8-7: *The City Map from ZombieMUD gives you an idea of the weirdness to come.*

Cyberpunk

Cyberpunk is a slippery term for the place where the worlds of high tech and low living meet. It's usually set in the not-so-distant future where today's trends have become tomorrow's nightmares.

The Sprawl

Addresses:

chiba.picosof.com 7777
165.227.31.2 7777

Classification: MOO

WWW: http://chiba.picosof.com:7777/

If you've read Chapter 5, you're probably pretty familiar with The Sprawl by now. However, if you're one of those impatient types who like to skim, you probably don't know that The Sprawl is one of the coolest places in Cyberspace. Taking its theme from the cyberpunk worlds of Snow Crash and Neuromancer, the world of the Chiba City Sprawl is a postmodern cyborg where technology meets the street. But don't feel restricted by the "cyber" theme—the creators of The Sprawl have endowed the characters with the ability to add their own creations to the world, so you never really know what lies beyond the next alley. In keeping with its futuristic theme, The Sprawl surfs the edge of MOO technology. Using the WOO Transaction Protocol developed at Picosof, you can interact with The Sprawl through the World Wide Web. In fact, you can even add your own Web links to The Sprawl, making this place not only a really cool world, but the first multimedia MOO.

Figure 8-8: *The logo from SenseMedia's* SenseMedia Surfer *online magazine, where you can look for the latest news on The Sprawl.*

Nuclearwar

Addresses:

Melba.Astrakan.HGS.SE 23

130.238.206.12 23

Classification: LPMud

WWW: http://www.astrakan.hgs.se/nuke/nuke.html

If you feel like kicking some mutant butt, or you harbor some secret wish to belong to an outlaw gang, then Nuclearwar might be the place to visit. Here, in a post-apocalyptic wasteland of the future, you're free from all those bothersome laws that restrict your real life, so you can live out all those anti-social fantasies without worrying about all the real-life gore and dirt. The world of Nuclearwar is pure anarchy—megacorps and gangs rule the earth in a free-wheeling fight to the finish. If death and pain sound like things you'd rather avoid, go play somewhere else, you pansy!

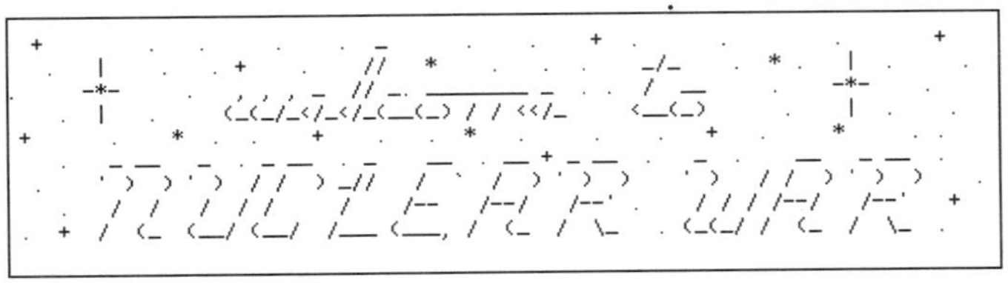

Figure 8-9: *Nuclearwar's opening screen only hints at what awaits...*

Sci-Fi

Fantastic places based on hard science and high fantasy, usually set in a future world and utilizing technology beyond our wildest dreams. Many science fiction worlds are based on sci-fi books and movies, so you may find a world that lets you live your favorite book!

Dune II

Addresses:

gardenia.berkeley.edu 4201

128.32.211.8 4201

Classification: MUSH

For more info: e-mail dune2@gardenia.berkeley.edu

WWW: http://www.ksu.ksu.edu:/~kxb/dune.html

If you enjoyed Frank Herbert's *Dune* series, you'll love Dune II, "Life in the Padishah Imperium." Just as heavy on the politics, economics and intrigue as the book series, Dune II thrusts you smack dab in the middle of the life of the Imperium, where you can find your fortune as a spice merchant or live out your life in obscurity as a wandering tribesman. Whatever your place in the society, you'll feel like you stepped right into the world of *Dune*.

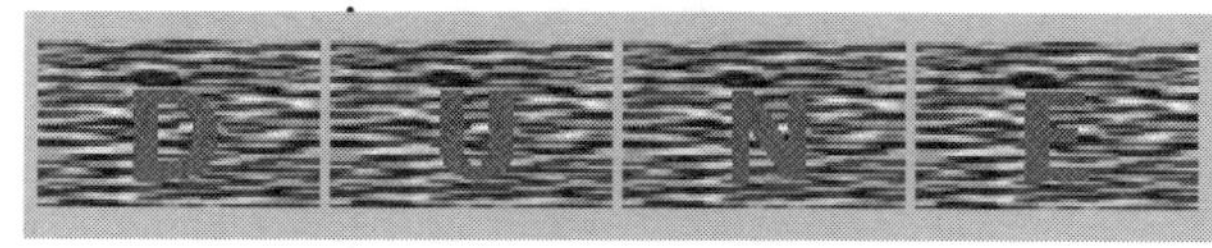

Figure 8-10: *The Dune logo from the DuneII MUSH home page.*

StarWars

Addresses:

starwars.wis.com 4402

199.3.240.54 4402

Classification: MUSH

A short time ago, in a computer not so far away, some very dedicated *Star Wars* fans created an incredible virtual version of the world of *Star Wars*. There are over 21 available races, dozens of parts for you to play, and all the intrigue, death and cut-throat trading that made *Star Wars* so much fun. If you can't wait for George Lucas to get off his tush and make a sequel, stop by the Star Wars MUSH and do it yourself. May the Force be with you!

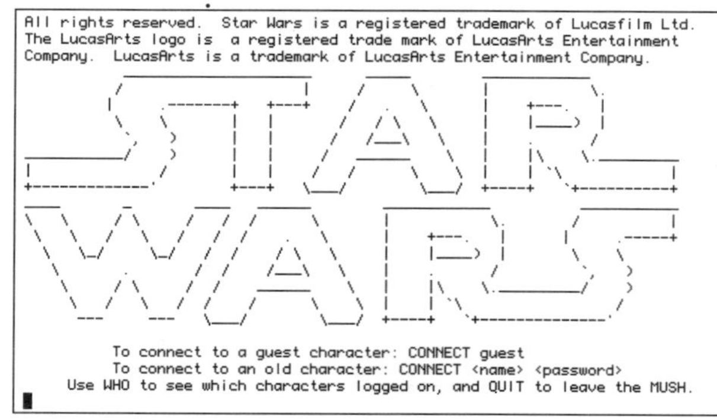

Figure 8-11: *It may not be the movies, but Star Wars' opening screen has the right idea.*

Alter Egos: Role Playing

You could say that all virtual worlds are a form of role playing, but the worlds designed specifically for role playing take things one step further. Generally, you are required to stay IC (in character) at all times, playing out the role that you have assumed.

Brazilian Dreams

Addresses:

red_panda.tbyte.com 4201

198.211.131.13 4201

Classification: MUCK

For more info: e-mail holmbeck@cs.weber.edu

If relaxing in an unspoiled rainforest glade and romping with your animal friends is something that you dream about, then Brazilian Dreams is your dream come true. Here, you can take the form of a rainforest creature or mythical beast and do just about anything your furry heart desires. Lay in the sun, romp with your rainforest pals or just kick back and listen to one of the many storytellers spin their tropical yarns.

Figure 8-12: *Self portrait of Telzey, one of the characters on FurryMUCK.*

FurryMUCK

Addresses:

sncils.snc.edu 8888

138.74.0.10 8888

Classification: MUCK

Register by e-mailing fmadmin@sncils.snc.edu

WWW: http://tachyon.qrc.com/~telzey/start.html

FurryMUCK is the premier furry place, a spot where you cast off the limitations and inhibitions of your boring human self and take the form of an animal. FurryMUCKers are a notoriously playful lot, so don't be surprised if you end up in a pile of fur, being tickled until you can't stand up! Because of the popularity of this world, you must e-mail the FurryMUCK higher-ups at fmadmin@sncils.snc.edu if you want a character, but if you just want to stop by and have a look, that's OK too.

Garou

Addresses:
cesium.clock.org 7000
130.43.2.43 7000
Classification: MUSH
WWW: http://nyx10.cs.du.edu:8001/~whartwel/garou.html

Figure 8-13: *This could be one of your friends on Garou MUSH.*

Vampires, werewolves and denizens of the dark meet regularly at the shadowy world of Garou MUSH. Chuck those Ann Rice novels out the window and quit paying 7 bucks a pop to see *Interview With a Vampire* for the zillionth time—visit Garou and live it! Based on the popular White Wolf gaming system, Garou MUSH is a world filled with werewolves, vampires and magic—all set in the place where our reality meets the shadow world. This is a place for serious role playing only, so if you want a character, you must e-mail garou-reg@cygnus.com with a character name, password and detailed background for your alter ego before you can enter as a regular player.

PernMUSH

Addresses:
sun.magic.ca 4201
199.166.230.69 4201
Classification: MUSH
For more info: get on the mailing list by sending the message
SUB pern-rp pername - firstname lastname
to listserv@cornell.edu
where pername= your character's name

If you've ever wondered what it would be like to leap on the back of a dragon and take to the skies of Pern, or just have a hankerin' to engage in some complex and satisfying role play, then PernMUSH may be for you. PernMUSH is a virtual world based on Anne McCaffrey's *Dragonriders of Pern* series where characters play the parts of dragonriders—brave souls who fly on the backs of dragons, the dominant life form of the planet Pern. Because McCaffery's novels straddle the worlds of fantasy and science fiction so well, they've always defied being categorized as either, which makes PernMUSH a much more interesting place. Worth a look.

Unbridled Desires

Addresses:

epona.magibox.net 8888

199.171.80.3 8888

Classification: MUCK

For more info: e-mail silkmare@pasture.magibox.net

WWW: http://www.warwick.ac.uk/~xuuaw/desires.html

If you were ever scolded as a child for engaging in too much horseplay, now you can thumb your nose at those stodgy old adults and play to your heart's content. Unbridled Desires is a unique MUSH where the players take equine form and horsing around is encouraged. You can be anything from a stodgy old mare to a flighty Pegasus, as long as you don't mind staying in character. If you've ever envied Black Beauty or longed to play the hairier part in *My Friend Flicka,* then Unbridled Desires should be your mane stop on the Net.

Figure 8-14: *An exuberant Unbridled Desires greeting on the UD home page is typical of the reception given to newbies.*

Hanging Out

These are places to kick back and shoot the breeze about anything that comes to mind. Usually, the theme of these worlds is secondary to an atmosphere that brings people together. If you want to meet some new friends or lounge around and chat with some old ones, these are the places to go.

BayMOO

Addresses:

baymoo.sfsu.edu 8888

130.212.41.251 8888

Classification: MOO

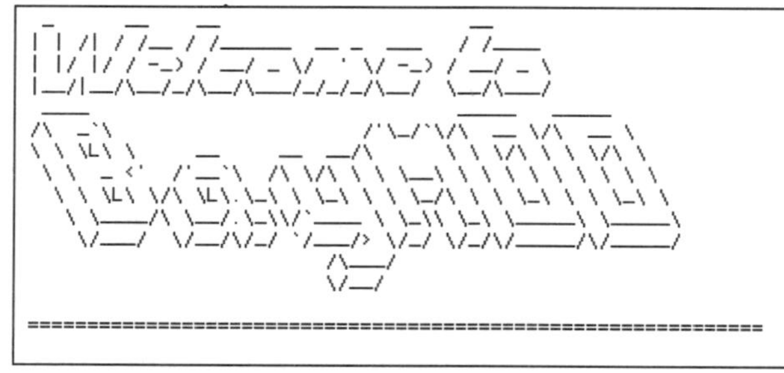

Figure 8-15: *Welcome to BayMOO!*

You may want to wear some flowers in your hair before you stop by BayMOO, but, man, do whatever feels right. BayMOO is a faithful Cyberspace reproduction of the San Francisco area but with additions that the city founders never dreamed of. You enter at the Aquatic Dome. From here, you can head off to the somewhat skewed Bay Area to visit past, present and future versions of SanFran, or you can head off to Netspace for some datasurfing or Other Worlds for a fantasy/sci-fi interlude. This is a young but rapidly growing place (*Wired* magazine even has its virtual cafe here, @go cafe wired when you log on) and it's hipper than you probably are. Groove on over and check it out.

Figure 8-16: *Hotwired's HotMOO link to BayMOO.*

Figure 8-17: *Libby, one of the friendly faces from GlobalMUSH.*

Global MUSH

Addresses:

lancelot.cif.rochester.edu 4201

128.151.220.22 4201

Classification: MUSH

WWW: http://lancelot.cif.rochester.edu/

GlobalMUSH is working hard to be all worlds to all people. Wanna hang out and chat? Go to the Conversation Room! Is urban life the place for you? Stop by the City! Want to go where no human has gone before? Space is not the only frontier here! Does hanging 10 sound good to you? There's a beautiful beach just a few keystrokes away. If none of these themes interests you, stop by anyway, because there are more than enough places to go around.

TimeMuse

Addresses:

murren.ai.mit.edu 4201

18.43.0.179 4201

Classification: MUSE

If you took a few Monty Python sketches, rolled them up with a few bad infomercials, a sprinkling of '50s sci-fi Z films, a dose of Mayberry and a pinch of Animaniacs, and whirled it all in a powerful pop culture blend-o-matic, then you'd probably end up with a mess. However, if you had the inspired genius of the creators of TimeMUSE, then you might end up with a glorious, inspired mess that's a heck of a fun place to visit! Here, you might enter a giant ChiaPet one minute, and the next you could find yourself playing spin the bottle with strangers, marching in a never-ending parade, or up to your neck in trouble at Spamedy Central. It's a weird, weird, world we live in—make it a little more fun and visit TimeMUSE.

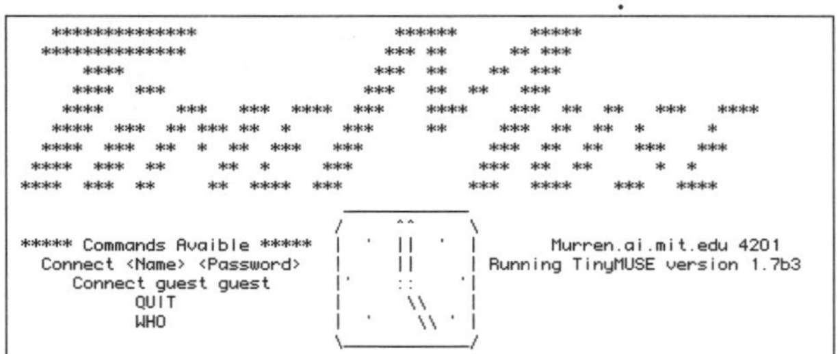

Figure 8-18: *The logon screen from TimeMUSE: pretty normal, but...*

TinyTim

Addresses:

myelin.uchc.edu 5440

155.37.1.251 5440

Classification: MUSH

WWW: http://www.tim.org/timalt/whatstim.html

I wouldn't be surprised if there's a tulip patch for you to tip-toe through here (though I didn't find it) because there's just about everything else in the world of TinyTim, the oldest MUSH in existence. It's a chatty, freewheeling, bizarre point-o-light in Cyberspace, and a darn good place to hang out and shoot the breeze with some people who are probably just as off-kilter as you are!

Figure 8-19: *Trout.Complex, Wizard of TinyTIM.*

The Fringe

The creme de la weird! Resisting description and maintaining a quirky humor all their own, virtual worlds on the fringes of reason often hide more than a few surprises. If you want to step off the beaten path, beat your own path to one of these worlds.

Figure 8-20: *Illuminati Online home page. Evidence of the conspiracy...*

Metaverse

Addresses:

metaverse.io.com 7777

199.170.88.12 7777

Classification: MOO

WWW: http://www.io.com/io/metaverse/

Illuminati Online is one of the hipster meccas on the Net, and Metaverse is its MOO. You'll find just about anything your twisted heart desires here, from the freewheeling capitalism of the Central Business District (with real shops!) to horror, gothic and adult areas sure to put some curl in your toes. However, don't confuse the Metaverse with any of those hippie drippy freebie lovefests that you might be used to on the Net—here, you gotta pay to play, though you can walk around for free to get a taste. Go check it out if you dare, but don't tell the Feds.

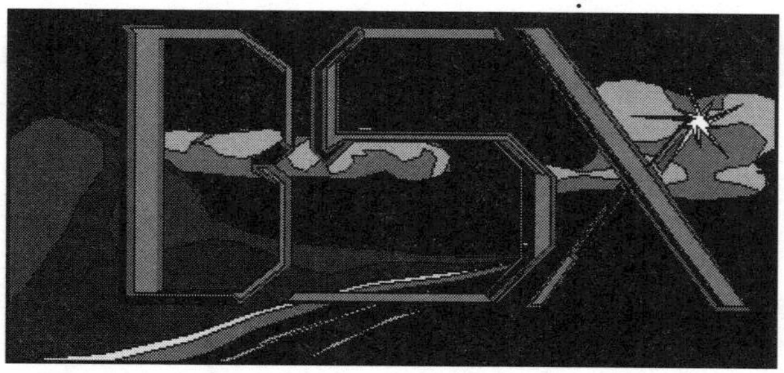

Figure 8-21: *The opening screen from Regenesis.*

Regenesis

Addresses:

birka.lysator.liu.se 7475

130.236.254.159 7475

Classification: BSX Mud

WWW: http://www.lysator.liu.se:7500/mud/bsxmud.html

Not only is Regenesis the only graphical MUD on the Net, it's a darn weird one at that! It's a strange world filled with Venusians, Martians and odd critters of several shapes, all rendered on your screen in living color. You can get to Regenesis though telnet or your usual MUD client, but the real fun begins when you ftp to ftp.lysator.liu.se / pub/lpmud/bsx and download the BSX client for your computer. As soon as you log on and see the pictures, you'll know you're in for a wild time!

Figure 8-22: *Grabbing a space cab to Mars.*

ZenMOO

Addresses:

cheshire.oxy.edu 7777

134.69.1.253 7777

Classification: MOO

For more info: e-mail t_pascal@oxy.edu

Guide available from:

ftp://pc4.math.oxy.edu:/pub/moo/zenmoo/zenguide.txt

Ahhh...as you enter ZenMOO, you are greeted by the swishing of saffron robes and the sweet attar of incense. As a cymbal chimes gently in the background, you know that you've arrived at a place of meditation and contemplation. A gently swirling tantric eddy in the electric pulse of the Net, ZenMOO is where you rush to do nothing with as little effort as possible. There would be high scores for the longest periods of meditation, but what's the point? To truly be at ZenMOO you may not need to visit at all.

Real Life Online

Where real-life pursuits meet online worlds. These are the more "practical" worlds that function as meeting centers, conference halls and virtual homes in Cyberspace for people who've extended their real life pursuits online. Perhaps a glimpse of things to come?

Diversity University

Addresses:

Moo.DU.org 8888

192.101.98.8 8888

Classification: MOO

WWW: http://pass.wayne.edu/DU.html

Strap on your virtual backpack and head on over to Diversity University to get your first taste of the school of the future. DU is the Net's first cyberschool, with classes, teachers, a student center, a library and even an inviting Quad where you can hang out and shoot the breeze with your fellow coeds. While you may not be able (yet) to get a degree here, DU is an interesting experiment in the future of learning. Besides, where else can you go to class in your pajamas if you want? For more info, go to the Diversity University home page at http://pass.wayne.edu/DU.html.

MediaMOO

Addresses:

purple-crayon.media.mit.edu 8888
18.85.0.48 8888

Classification: MOO

What began as an experiment in text-based virtual reality has become the hangout for a virtual who's who of media researchers. The MediaMOO is an online recreation of MIT's Media Lab, and it's populated exclusively by people interested in the future of interactive communication, alternative media and virtual reality. Not that it's a stodgy place, though—these folks are a pretty creative lot and you'll find just about anything you can imagine here from autonomous robots to pour you a beer to poetry readings, online conferences and a ubiquitous train to haul you around. Stop by as a guest and see for yourself what some of the top minds on the Net can do when they get together in one place.

Figure 8-23: *Stop reading this book and head out into the virtual universe!*

Appendix A
About the Online Companion

Welcome to the *Internet Virtual Worlds Online Companion!*

Got the travel bug? Want to know more about virtual worlds? Well don't stop with this book. The *Internet Virtual Worlds Online Companion* gives you a never-ending source of valuable information for your virtual travels.

Ventana offers an *Online Companion* for the *Internet Virtual Worlds Quick Tour* as part of the Ventana Visitor's Center. The *Online Companion* includes all the software mentioned in the *Quick Tour*, with the latest versions accessible as soon as they are made available, along with version change notes; Chapter 8, the online virtual world listings; and Ventana's own virtual world, the Internet Meta-MUD, the MUD of MUDs. There is also an online guide that will provide you with quick access to Internet resources related to this book. The *Internet Virtual Worlds Quick Tour Online Companion* will help make this book dynamic, up-to-date and continually useful.

The *Internet Virtual Worlds Online Companion* also links you to the Ventana Library where you will find useful press and jacket information as well as other Ventana Press offerings. Plus you have access to a wide selection of exciting new releases and coming attractions. In addition, Ventana's Online Library allows you to order online the books you want.

The *Internet Virtual Worlds Online Companion* represents Ventana Online's ongoing commitment to offering the most dynamic and exciting products possible. And soon Ventana Online will be adding more services, including more multimedia supplements, searchable indices and sections of the book reproduced and hyperlinked to the Internet resources they reference.

To access, connect via the World Wide Web to http://www.vmedia.com/ivwqt.html

GLOSSARY

AC Short for "Armor Class." Your character's armor class indicates how hard you are to damage.

Admin One or more people who are in charge of the actual running of a world (the administrators). Admins usually maintain the program, arbitrate disputes between characters and oversee the physical care of the machine the world runs on.

AFK Short for "Away from Keyboard." Used to indicate to other players that you are stepping away for a minute to take care of real-life demands.

Alias Abbreviation for another command. For example, the command "get all from corpse" may be shortened to "gac." Aliases can be defined either on the world or with a client program.

Bot Short for "robot." A bot is a program designed to act like a real character. You'll often find bots on virtual worlds that allow players to program their own objects.

BRB Short for "Be Right Back." BRB indicates that you must temporarily step away and take care of something in real life. See **AFK**.

Bug A mistake or problem in the program that runs the virtual world. The term "bug" originated with computing pioneer Admiral Grace Hopper who told a story about a problem with one of the first computers (the Harvard Mark II) that was solved when a technician found a moth in the internal wiring. For a while, the moth (the original "bug") was on display at the Naval Surface Warfare Center.

Character Your online alter ego. When you interact in a virtual world, you do so though a character you create with its own sex, description and abilities. If you are on a competitive gaming world, your character rises in status by accumulating points awarded for fulfilling tasks and killing monsters.

Class A general way to group characters based on abilities, interests and attributes. Often, when you create a new character on a gaming world, you must specify a class for that character such as Mage, Warrior, Thief or Cleric. Each class has its own unique abilities, attributes and limitations.

Client A program used to connect to and interact with a virtual world. Generally, a client runs on your computer or your host computer and is used to connect to virtual worlds. The simplest client is telnet, which allows you to connect to the remote computer that a virtual world runs on and provides few extra features. However, specialized MUD or MOO client programs allow you to define aliases, log sessions to a file, set triggers and even assist you in your mapping.

Coding Programming your own creations on a virtual world. On some worlds, only high-level characters or wizards are given the ability to add new areas or objects to the world. However, other worlds (usually MOOs, MUCKs and MUSHes) allow all players to program their own objects.

Crash A crash is a catastrophic error in the program running the world or the computer that the world runs on. When a world crashes, it usually must be taken off-line until the problem is corrected. If you are on a world when it crashes, you can expect to lose everything you've done since you logged on.

Cyberspace Word coined by sci-fi writer William Gibson to refer to a near future computer network where users can mentally travel through matrices of data. The term is now often used to describe today's Internet.

Cyborg A term used to describe the combination of a person and a computer. It's quite common in science fiction. On a virtual world, it usually describes a character who makes heavy use of triggers and other client features to do things more quickly than an unaided human could.

Dial-up connection A connection from your computer to a host Internet-connected computer over standard phone lines. Dial-up is currently the most popular form of Net connection for the home user.

DikuMUD A type of MUD designed as a compromise between fighting and social interaction. The DIKU in DikuMUD comes from an acronym for Datalogisk Institut ved Kbenhavns Universitet, the Department of Computer Science at the University of Copenhagen, where DikuMUD was developed. Probably the most popular form of MUD on the Internet.

Dino Slang for someone who's been on a virtual world or in the virtual world scene for a long time. Short for "dinosaur."

Direct connection A connection between your computer system and the Internet. When you use a direct connection, your computer becomes a part of the Internet network and you must use programs on your own computer (rather than a host computer) to access the Net. A direct connection can be made permanently through a dedicated line leased from the phone company (at a high price) or temporarily using a SLIP or PPP connection over regular phone lines.

Experience points As you complete tasks or kill monsters on a virtual world, you are rewarded with a number of points proportionate to the difficulty of the task. As you accumulate points, your character attains higher levels.

FAQ Frequently Asked Question. Can be used to describe a common newbie question or a text file on the Internet that answers common questions on a given subject. FAQs are a major source of Net knowledge and wisdom.

Flags Attributes of a room or object on a world that can be set by the person coding that object or place.

Flame An excessively angry or irrational response to someone. Newbies are often flamed for asking what others perceive to be stupid questions that have been answered in the FAQs. Generally, there's no excuse for flaming someone else. The best tactic to use if someone irritates you is to ignore them.

Frob A command that is used to change a character's level. Often used to request a higher level for a character based on the fact that the character has a high level on another world. When a world offers "frobbing," it means that the admins will give your new character a higher level if you are a wizard on another world.

FTP An abbreviation for file transfer protocol. FTP can be used as a noun to describe the protocol used to transfer files from one computer to another across the Internet, or as a verb to describe the act of transferring files (e.g. "I'm going to ftp that client program from Lysator").

Furry A genre of role playing where people assume the roles of animals. Furries can also be characters that combine human and animal characteristics. Furry worlds are usually fun loving, mischievous places.

God Someone who has attained a sufficiently high level as to become immortal on a virtual world. Also used to describe the people in charge of running the world. See **Wizard**.

Guild A group of characters of similar class. Guilds are the online version of professional organizations and are often formed to provide training for low-level characters, places where characters with similar interests and attributes can meet and chat, and a way of grouping characters for a common cause.

Haven A safe room where players cannot be killed. The room where you first arrive is usually a haven.

Hit points A number that indicates how much damage your character can take before getting killed. Usually expressed as a ratio of the number of current hit points over the maximum number of hit points you have, e.g., 25/50.

Host The computer that you use when you are utilizing a dial-up account. If you are using a host computer, you access the Internet though programs that you run on the host computer, such as telnet or FTP.

IC Short for "in character." When you are on a role-playing world, you are expected to behave in a way consistent with your character's attributes, interests and description. If you want to discuss your latest exam or world events, you can go out of character (OOC) and discuss these real-life concerns in special OOC rooms away from the main part of the world.

Immort Used to describe someone who has attained high enough status to become immortal (unkillable) on a virtual world. Often, someone who has become immortal becomes a god or a wizard.

Internet, The The worldwide network of computers connected though a TCP/IP network. The Internet was originally set up as a way for researchers at different universities to share information. It has grown exponentially in the last few years to connect about a million computers and several million users across the planet. See **Cyberspace**.

IP address A number assigned to any Internet-connected computer. Usually, you can use either an IP address or a name address to access a computer across the Net. For example, BatMUD's name address is bat.cs.hut.fi, but its IP address is 130.233.40.180.

Kill A character is usually considered killed when his or her hit points drop below a set level. A character who is killed usually loses all equipment that he or she is holding. On some worlds, when a character is killed, it is gone forever, while on other worlds that character can begin again but must take an experience point or level penalty. Also see **Playerkilling**, **Experience points**, **Level** and **Hit points**.

Lag A noticeable slowness occurring when many people try to connect to a world at the same time, or when a world is connected to the Internet though a slow-speed connection.

Level A numeric indication of a character's status on a virtual world. Each level your character attains increases his or her attributes, hit points and abilities. See **Experience points**.

Logging Capturing text that appears on your screen to a text file so you can review it later.

LPC A language used on LPMuds to code new areas or monsters. Based on the C programming language.

LPMud The first type of virtual world that allowed players to program new areas using its own internal programming language. LPMud is named after its creator, Lars Pensjö, and is one of the most popular types of virtual worlds.

Mana Most often used on DikuMUDs, mana is usually a number indicating how much magic a character can use. Each spell that a character casts reduces the amount of mana available.

Map A drawing that you create to keep track of where your character has been on a virtual world. Learning how to make a good map is one of the key skills you need to develop if you're into MUDs.

Mob A slang term for "mobiles" or monsters on a virtual world. Monsters are non-player characters who roam the world. Often, players reach a higher level by fighting and killing monsters.

Monster see **Mob**.

MOO An acronym for MUD, Object Oriented. MOOs are types of virtual worlds where characters can program their own places and objects. The original MOO is Lambda MOO, created by Pavel Curtis at the Xerox Palo Alto Research Center. MOOs are almost exclusively social environments where people meet to chat and build.

MUCK A pun on the word MUD. MUCKs are usually social worlds where people can build their own objects. Originally developed by Stephen White.

MUD An acronym for Multi User Dungeon or Multi User Domain. Originally, it was the name for the first text-based virtual reality developed by Roy Trubshaw in 1979 at Essex University. MUD is now used as a general term for all virtual worlds, though because of its connotations to game-like worlds, others have suggested MU** as a better way to refer to all online worlds.

MUDlist A list of online worlds' names and addresses. Some virtual worlds make a MUDlist available online. Often you can find mudlists posted to one of the many virtual world-related newsgroups.

MUSH MUSH stands for Multi User Shared Hallucination, a virtual world system developed by Larry Foard in an effort to increase social interaction and give players greater programming abilities. MUSHes are usually social or role-playing worlds.

Net See **Internet, The** and **Cyberspace**.

Newbie A term used to describe people new to online worlds and, in general, new to the Internet. Newbie can be a put-down or a simple description, depending on the context.

Newsgroup An Internet discussion group.

Object An item on a virtual world that characters can interact with. On a MOO, object is used to describe any part of the world that characters can do things with, including rooms and bots.

OOC Short for "out of character." On a role-playing world, players are expected to act "in character" at all times, behaving as the character they are playing would. If characters must discuss something from real life or have questions about the workings of the world, then they can move to special OOC rooms where such discussions are allowed. Consistently breaking character on a role-playing world is considered a serious breach of etiquette.

Operating system The software that takes care of all the details of making a computer run and providing an interface for the user. UNIX, VMS, Windows and the MacOS are all examples of operating systems.

Password A secret word that you use to gain access to your computer account or virtual world character.

Player Can be used interchangeably with character as a way of referring to a person's virtual world alter ego. Player can also be used to describe the person playing the character on a virtual world.

Playerkilling The act of killing another character. Killing other players is allowed only on certain worlds, and you should check the rules of the world you are on before you engage in any wanton slaughter. Also see **Haven**.

Port A number indicating what part of a remote computer you are trying to connect to. Virtual worlds usually have their own port number to set them apart from the general login section of their host computer. If you try to connect to a virtual world and get a prompt that says something like "Login:" or "User Name:" you probably forgot to use the world's port number.

Pose A way of communicating with other players using non-verbal communication. Posing is a way of indicating actions such as smiling, laughing, dancing and so on, and is a very important part of online communication. Learning to pose effectively can make talking to other people a lot of fun.

PPP (Point-to-Point Protocol) A type of Internet connection where a computer can use phone lines and a modem to connect to the Internet (without having to connect to a host). You must use PPP software to establish the connection. PPP connections are rented from a local Internet service provider. See **SLIP** and **Direct connection**.

Quest A puzzle or series of puzzles that must be solved in order to reach a goal. Quests also usually involve conquering a monster, saving a damsel in distress or finding a special item. Upon successfully completing a quest, your character is awarded a certain number of experience points.

Quota The limit imposed by a virtual world on how many objects a player can build.

Race What species a character belongs to. Mainly appearing on fantasy or science fiction worlds, a character's race determines the base physical characteristics and abilities that character has. Often, race is also tied to class, so that characters of certain races are prevented from choosing one or more classes.

Real life What you spend your time doing when you aren't online. Ultimately much more important.

Register Some virtual worlds require that you send e-mail to the admins when requesting a character. This process is known as "registering" your new character with the world.

Rent On many worlds, when you leave a game session, you lose all the equipment you had accumulated. Renting allows you to pay for the privilege of saving all the stuff that your character has accumulated so that you don't have to find it all again when you come back. Usually, you rent a room in an inn for a set number of gold pieces per day.

rl Short for real life. See **Real life**.

Role Playing Taking the form and assuming all the characteristics and behaviors of a certain character. On role-playing worlds, the idea is to behave just like your character in an effort to create a world as real and as rich as real life. Role-playing worlds are usually very serious about having players that are committed to their roles. These worlds often require prospective players to submit detailed backgrounds, descriptions and character sketches before they will be admitted. See also **IC**, **OOC**, **Real life** and **Register**.

Sex Your character's gender. Can be male, female, neuter or other depending on the world.

Shell account see **Dial-up connection**.

SLIP (Serial Line Internet Protocol) A type of Internet connection where a computer can use phone lines and a modem to connect to the Internet (without having to connect to a host). You must use SLIP software to establish the connection. SLIP connections are rented from a local Internet service provider.

Spamming Taken from the classic Monty Python skit where the word "spam" is repeated ad nauseam. Spamming refers to the act of spouting useless, boring or annoying words while online. On a virtual world, someone who insists on shouting about everything they do is considered to be spamming.

Squid tank The computer room where people meet to go online together. E.g., "Did you see all those people in the squid tank last night? They must have been on that MUD for eight hours!"

Telnet An application that lets you log into another system using the telnet protocol. Also see **Client**.

TinySex Simulated sexual activity done on a virtual world. Like the text equivalent of phone sex. It should be entered into with caution because you never know who's who online, and some people love enticing a person into an extended TinySex session and then posting a log of the activity to various newsgroups.

Toading Often the ultimate punishment for a character who insists on being annoying, harasses other players or seriously breaks one of the rules of the online world. If a character is toaded, it loses its characteristics, property and experience, and is permanently described as an ugly, slimy toad. Sometimes, toaded characters are confined to a public place so that they can serve as a warning to others.

Triggers Some clients offer this special feature, which allows a person to program pre-set responses so that the client automatically responds to the online world. Triggers are useful anywhere fast reflexes are useful, especially fights. See **Cyborg**.

URL Uniform Resource Locator. The addressing system used in the World Wide Web and a proposed addressing standard for the entire Internet. The URL contains information about the method of access, the server to be accessed and the path of any files to be accessed.

Verb A word or command that an object responds to. See **Object** and **MOO**.

Virtual reality A computer system that creates the illusion, either through graphical representation or textual description, of another world or reality. See **Virtual world**.

Virtual world A text-based virtual reality located on a computer connected to the global Internet. Virtual worlds are places where people can meet and interact online in a spatially represented environment. Virtual worlds use textual descriptions to create, as Howard Rheingold says, "the illusion of being immersed in an artificial world, or of being present in a remote location in the physical world." These illusions can take the form of games, meeting centers, conference halls or just a local coffee shop, but the major factor is that virtual worlds allow people to share these illusions.

Web see **World Wide Web**.

Wizard Someone who has attained a high enough level on a world to become immortal, or someone involved with the actual running of the world. See **God** and **Immort**.

World Wide Web A hypermedia document presentation system that can accessed over the Internet using software called a browser, such as Mosaic or Netscape. Also called the Web, or WWW. See **URL**.

INDEX

A

B

C

D

E

F

G

H

I

J

K

L

M

N

O

P

Q

R

S

W

Z

COLOPHON

This book was developed on a Power Macintosh 8100. All pages were produced in Aldus PageMaker 5.0. Some graphics were edited using Adobe Photoshop 3.0. Chapter titles are set in Anna. The body text is set in Palatino. Subheads, sidebars and tables are set in varying weights of Futura. The title of the book (on the cover and title pages) is set in Michelangelo. Page proofs were output to a Hewlett-Packard LaserJet 4M Plus. Final film output was produced using a Linotronic 330.

Netscape Quick Tour

Macintosh Version: $14.00, 184 pages, illustrated
Windows Version: $14.00, 192 pages, illustrated

The latest "killer app" to storm the Internet allows for greater throughput and continuous document streaming, letting users start reading a Web page as soon as it begins to load. This jumpstart for Netscape introduces its handy toolbar, progress indicator and built-in image decompressor to everyday Net surfers, letting them make the most of this streamlined software. A basic Web overview is spiced with listings of the authors' favorite sights—and sounds—on the World Wide Web.

Internet E-Mail Quick Tour

$14.00, 152 pages, illustrated

Whether it's the Internet or an online service, most people use their connections primarily for electronic messaging. This all-in-one guide to getting it right includes tips on software, security, style and etiquette. Also included: how to obtain an e-mail account, useful addresses, interesting mailing lists and more!

Internet Chat Quick Tour

$14.00, 200 pages, illustrated

Global conversations in real-time are an integral part of the Internet. The worldwide chat network is where users find online help and forums on the latest scientific research. The *Internet Chat Quick Tour* describes the best software sites for users to chat on a variety of subjects and shows users where to take out verbal aggression.

Books marked with this logo include a free Internet *Online Companion™*, featuring archives of free utilities plus a software archive and links to other Internet resources.

Voodoo Windows

$19.95, 312 pages, illustrated

Work Windows wizardry with productivity-enhancing tips. Organized by subject, this book offers a wealth of Windows techniques, shortcuts and never-before-published tricks that will streamline your daily tasks and save time. A great reference for beginners and experienced users alike.

The Windows Shareware 500

$39.95, 456 pages, illustrated

The best Windows shareware available, from among thousands of contenders. Includes utilities, sounds, fonts, icons, games, clip art, multimedia and more. **BONUS:** Four companion disks: three that feature top-rated programs and an America Online membership disk. Includes 10 hours free online time (for new members only)!

The Visual Guide to Visual Basic for Windows, Second Edition

$29.95, 1292 pages, illustrated

An A-to-Z examination of every command and technique in Microsoft's landmark GUI language, including functions, illustrations and suggested uses for each. Fully updated for Version 3.0, it offers users at all levels insight on customizing Windows and creating useful applications that look professional and perform efficiently. With more than 600 illustrations, it is truly the classic reference for Microsoft's bestselling language.

Check your local bookstore or software retailer for these and other bestselling titles, or call toll free: 800/743-5369

FOR MAC & WINDOWS

Walk the Web!

Tour the best of the best. Shannon Turlington takes you on a memorable trip to more than 300 exciting Web sites. With in-depth descriptions of why each one is special, Turlington shows how easy it is to visit and enjoy these innovative, engaging and informative sites!

Full text on CD-ROM—browse at your leisure off-line. Then when you've plotted your trip, log on and use this hyperlinked version of *Walking the World Wide Web* to point and click your way to the world's most exciting sites.

Free! One-year subscription to *Online Companion*™—a full online version of *Walking the World Wide Web* residing on Ventana Online™, featuring updates and new additions regularly—**a $19.95 value!**

Ventana Online also provides free instant access to the latest versions of all the free software mentioned in *Walking the World Wide Web*—including updates and change notes, the moment they are available. All with point-and-click convenience, in a friendly format for Mac and Windows.

$29.95, 360 pages, illustrated.